Strength in Numbers

Quarter by Quarter with the Green Bay Packers

Members of the 1942 Green Bay Packers pose for this photo at the City Stadium practice field. The Joannes Park baseball grandstand is visible in the background. (L to R) Baby Ray, Don Hutson, Charley Brock, Cecil Isbell, Lou Brock, Tony Canadeo, Buckets Goldenberg, Joe Laws (front and center), Pete Tinsley, Andy Uram, Bill Kuusisto, Russ Letlow, Larry Craig, Ernie Pannell and Bill Lee. (Photo courtesy of the Green Bay Press-Gazette)

Eric Goska

M&B Global Solutions Inc.
Green Bay, Wisconsin (USA)

Strength in Numbers

Quarter by Quarter with the Green Bay Packers

© 2019 Eric Goska

First edition
All Rights Reserved with the exception of quoting brief passages for the purpose of review. No part of this publication may be reproduced or utilized in any other form or by any means, electronic or mechanical, including photocopying, recording, or by any information storage and retrieval system without the permission of the publisher, M&B Global Solutions, Inc.

Disclaimer
The views expressed in this work are solely those of the author and do not necessarily reflect the views of the publisher, and the publisher hereby disclaims any responsibility for them. In the event you use any of the information in this book for yourself, which is your constitutional right, the author and the publisher assume no responsibility for your actions.

All text, photographs and artwork are the property of the author unless otherwise noted or credited. All trademarks, personal and brand names, modes and numbers, and other product designations and statistical data referred to herein are the property of their respective owners and are used solely for identification/reference purposes. In the event you use any of the information in this book for yourself, which is your constitutional right, the author and the publisher assume no responsibility for your actions.

Front cover photo – David Bakhtiari hoists Randall Cobb to celebrate his 3-yard touchdown catch from Aaron Rodgers during the Packers' 38-17 victory over the Carolina Panthers on October 19, 2014, at Lambeau Field. *(Photo courtesy of the Green Bay Press-Gazette)*

ISBN-13: 978-1-942731-36-8
ISBN-10: 1-942731-36-1

Published by M&B Global Solutions Inc.
Green Bay, Wisconsin (USA)

Dedication

For the Goose Goose Girls:

Ann, Nicole, and Rebecca

Forever will you live in my heart.

Contents

Foreword 1
Introduction 3
A Few Words About Play-by-Plays 5
Acknowledgements 9

First Quarter 11
    First Impressions—Don Hutson 13
    First Quarter—November 12, 1967 15
    Rushing—Jim Taylor 17
    Receiving—James Lofton 21
    Passing—Aaron Rodgers 25
    Scoring—Weert Engelmann 29

Second Quarter 33
    Second Quarter—November 9, 2014 35
    Rushing—John Brockington 39
    Receiving—Don Hutson 43
    Passing—Brett Favre 47
    Scoring—Ryan Longwell 51

Halftime 55
    Half-Life Rushing—Ahman Green 56
    Half-Life Receiving—Bill Howton 58

Third Quarter 61
    Third Quarter—November 23, 1997 63
    Rushing—Tony Canadeo 67
    Receiving—Antonio Freeman 71
    Passing—Bart Starr 75
    Scoring—Mason Crosby 79

Contents

Fourth Quarter 83
    Fourth Quarter—October 17, 1983 85
    Rushing—Ahman Green 87
    Receiving—Donald Driver 91
    Passing—Don Majkowski 95
    Scoring—Paul Hornung 99
    Lasting Impressions—Final Plays 103
    Instant Replay—November 5, 1989 104

OT—Other Topics 109
    Down and Distant 111
    All-Positive 100s 115
    Fail-Safe 100s 119
    Chain-Moving 100s 123
    The Powerball is 10 127
    The Whole Enchilada 131
    Catch of Characters 135
    Fourth-and-Six 139

Lists 143
    All-Time Rushing 144
    All-Time Receiving 149
    All-Time Passing 154
    Scoring Leaders 157

About the Author 161

Foreword

By Bob McGinn

Year after year, the Green Bay Packers attract more fans to their world-wide following, and with them comes more revenue than even the Packers, at times, quite know what to do with.

The big names draw the cheers and make the headlines. In my 40 years of covering the organization, however, it's the little-known, behind-the-scenes people who did and are doing their jobs beautifully that left the most indelible impression on me.

Carol Edwin, an unforgettably friendly presence, at the main switchboard. Gentlemanly Domenic Gentile heading the training room. The ever-smiling Mark Wagner in the ticket department. Shirley Leonard, an all-time sweetheart, in public relations. Tireless Bryan Nehring in the equipment room and on the practice field. The kindly combination of Darlene Kramer, Margaret Meyers and Jeanne Bruette in the GM's office. Hard-bitten college scouts such as Tom Tipps and Bobo Cegelski. Genial Phil Pionek in the executive wing.

Which brings me to Eric Goska, the unassuming, self-styled "stats" guy whose newest book is in your hands.

Eric is one of those largely anonymous faces that many Packers fans wouldn't recognize. The fact is that the Packers as a franchise couldn't have been more fortunate to have the league's pre-eminent independent historian/statistician/author chronicling them.

I met Eric in 1986 at the *Green Bay Press-Gazette*. I was starting my 11th year at the newspaper and third as the full-time Packers beat writer. He had just been hired to work part-time in the sports department.

It wasn't long before I came to understand the gold mine of information we had just brought on board.

Eric Goska

After home and road games, one of my first calls usually was to Eric. I'd inquire about possible statistical milestones or oddities, and within minutes he would answer my question and usually offer many more tidbits.

At the time, the Packers media guide was incomplete, to say the least. Computers were prehistoric. The Internet wasn't.

Lee Remmel, the team's beloved director of public relations, opened his door and files to Eric, who by then was hell-bent on becoming the authority on Packers statistics. Eric remembers sitting in the cramped public relations office near Leonard's desk, copying game scoresheets by hand from the 1940s and 1950s.

In the summer of 1989, Shirley Leonard wrote a letter to Elias Sports Bureau requesting permission for Eric to continue his research into all things Packers in a visit to its offices in New York. Eric vividly remembers copying those leather helmet-era scoresheets with nary a bathroom break and until his hand cramped.

His research would bring him to the Pro Football Hall of Fame, to NFL Films, and to St. Louis, where team publicists graciously allowed him to copy some missing Packers-Rams games from the late 1940s and 1950s.

In the early 1990s, Eric shared his precious data with Remmel, and the result was a substantial overhaul of the Packers record book.

Befitting his background as a mathematics graduate of Northwestern University, suffice it to say that Eric is one of the most precise people I have encountered. His approach to football statistics is of the highest standard. He is dogged in obtaining information, meticulous in developing it, and ever mindful that mistakes in his field cannot be tolerated.

Eric's first two books on the Packers were invaluable works that told the statistical story of the franchise season by season. They've never been farther away than a swivel of my office chair.

Now I have a feeling Eric's latest undertaking will fall into the same, indispensable category. For the first time, one can find quarter-by-quarter numbers for the Packers in several areas, and in the second half of the book you'll find essays in which Eric shares his fresh views on the Packers by the numbers.

As a subscriber to *The Sporting News* during my adolescent years, I can recall Damon Runyan using the nickname "Figure Filbert" for Ernest Lanigan, the leading baseball statistician of his time. Runyan might have used "Numbers Nut."

Eric Goska is all of that and more when it comes to football in Green Bay over the last 100 years. Enjoy his painstaking research and this terrific book.

Bob McGinn is a sportswriter covering the Packers for the Green Bay Press-Gazette *from 1979-'90,* The Milwaukee Journal *from 1991-'94,* The Milwaukee Journal Sentinel *from 1995-2016, and BobMcGinnFootball.com since 2017. He is the author of* The Ultimate Super Bowl Book. *In 2011, he was honored with the Dick McCann Memorial Award for long and distinguished reporting on pro football.*

Introduction

I am different.

I am not on social media. I do not own a cell phone.

Wisconsin born and raised, I've never used a snowblower.

When game day arrives, some fans paint their faces. Others disappear into an alter ego.

I crunch numbers. It's what I do.

Bob Wolfley of *The Milwaukee Journal-Sentinel* labeled my hobby a "preoccupation." Dick Schaap referred to one of my statistics as "arcane" on page 40 of his book, *Green Bay Replay*.

It's reassuring to get noticed.

In your hands you hold a different way of looking at Green Bay Packers history. It wouldn't have been possible if I were the type to follow a well-worn path.

More than 30 years of information gathering has led here. I have play-by-plays for roughly 95 percent of all Packers games (see the next section). Every available offensive play for the team has been entered into Excel spreadsheets.

Sorting those numbers can lead to some surprises. Floyd (Breezy) Reid is the only Packer to have rushed for 100 yards in the fourth quarter of a game. All but two of Keith Woodside's 144 career receptions came on first and second downs.

Breaking down statistics by quarter or down or some other grouping has become big in sports. It is called splitting. The number of categories into which numbers can be assembled (by month, playing surface or opponent) is limited only by one's imagination.

Splits are available at espn.com as far back as 1993. Unfortunately, nothing is available for the 70-plus years before that.

That's a gaping hole. Big enough to serve as the genesis for this book.

Wouldn't it be interesting to see how Don Hutson's second-quarter receiving numbers stack up against those of others who wore the green and gold? Might it be informative to know which Green Bay quarterbacks were the most productive in the game's final 15 minutes?

Eric Goska

The story of the Green Bay Packers has been told and retold. Until now, it has never been presented as a game would unfold; that is, quarter-by-quarter. Unless otherwise noted, the information in this book pertains to the regular season only.

We'll examine four offensive areas: rushing, receiving, passing and scoring. We'll break down each by quarter, and then determine who the career, season and game leaders were for each of those 15-minute periods.

After that, we'll head into OT (Other Topics). A series of essays will spotlight a variety of subjects, some never before contemplated.

We'll wrap up with a few lists. For the first time ever, the top 50 scorers in Packers history will have their life's work segmented by quarter (and overtime, if applicable).

This, then, has been my calling – to determine firsts, mosts, lasts, and bests – and share what I discover. It's what I love to do.

And in that, perhaps, I am not so different after all.

~ Eric Goska

A Few Words About Play-by-Plays

Official scorers shall be appointed by the Commissioner's office.

Official score sheets shall be compiled after the game by transcribing play-by-play accounts recorded by the official scorer during the progress of the contest.

Official scorers shall retain their play-by-play accounts until the end of the season.

In the 1940s and 1950s, the instructions above were always the first encountered in the Scoring Rules section of the NFL's Record and Rules Manuals. Innocuous enough at the time, the directive to hold on to play-by-play accounts only until the end of the season was one that lacked foresight.

From a researcher's standpoint, those documents should have been safeguarded until the end of time. By failing to preserve those play-by-play accounts, invaluable information was lost. Much of the data is likely gone forever.

Because of this, only a handful of NFL teams can provide relatively complete accounting for games played prior to 1960. The Detroit Lions have some play-by-plays from the early 1950s. The Rams can go back to the late 1940s.

The Packers? The first season from which a majority survives is 1959, the year Vince Lombardi became the team's coach and general manager.

In Green Bay, fortunately, one need not rely solely on the team and league. Others have preserved some of the rich history of this unique franchise.

The Green Bay Press-Gazette

The newspaper published play-by-plays after most games from 1923 through 1940. Some, authored by sports editor John Walter in the mid- to late 1930s, may have been those the league relied upon, as Walter's numbers from them often line up with what is found on official scoresheets.

Even so, many of these game accounts are problematic, especially the farther back one goes. The names of passers were occasionally omitted. Lines of scrimmage were sometimes given as merely a number minus any designation as to which side of the field a team was on.

Despite those limitations, much information can be gleaned. Fred (OJ) Larson intercepted at least one pass in a team-record six consecutive games in 1925. Larson doesn't get his due without the newspaper documenting, in detail, what happened in those games.

Art Daley

Art Daley kept handwritten play-by-plays – with an assist from Dave Yuenger and Lee Remmel – from 1942 through 1968. This affable gentleman began his career with the *Press-Gazette* in November 1941 and was named sports editor in June 1946.

Daley had the presence of mind to list a player's name rather than his jersey number when scribbling down what he saw on the field. This eliminated potential confusion – was that a 3 or an 8, a 21 or a 27? – and it saved time. There is no need to search for old rosters to match players with numbers.

The biggest drawback? Daley's work is not official. Apparently no one called out distances in the press box then as is done now. His totals can be off by a few yards because of this.

Still, without Daley's note taking, we likely would not know that on November 11, 1945, the Rams' Jim Gillette ended three consecutive Packers' drives by intercepting the same passer – Roy McKay – each time. Tossing interceptions to end three straight advances is frustrating enough. Having each wind up in the arms of the same player might lead one to believe he is cursed.

NFL Films

There is more to NFL Films than highlight reels and bloopers. Occasionally, complete or nearly complete recordings of games from the 1940s and 1950s can be found.

Compiling a play-by-play from game film takes patience and dedication. But with the aid of an official scoresheet and one or more newspaper accounts, it can be done.

As with the other sources mentioned, numbers won't always be spot-on. A play or two might go missing when the camera operator had to change film.

Still, what results after winding and rewinding the tape can be illuminating. Lou Brock – not Charley Brock – made the Packers' only interception against the Detroit Lions in the 1945 finale despite what the league manual says. Jack Jacobs did not throw five interceptions against the New York Giants in 1947 – Tony Canadeo tossed the fifth – but those who scored the game got it wrong.

These sources – the *Green Bay Press-Gazette*, Art Daley and NFL Films – proved invaluable. And yet some play-by-plays remain impossible to obtain.

Official Play-by-Plays

Prior to the use of computers, "official" did not always mean error-free. Play-by-plays from the 1980s and before occasionally contain mistakes.

One of the biggest occurred on October 2, 1983. Tampa Bay's Frank Garcia, who led the NFC in punting average that year (42.2), was shortchanged by 22 yards when he visited Lambeau Field. His true average that season on 95 punts was 42.4.

Ken Payne's longest catch in 1975 was 57 yards, not 54. Against the Giants that year, Payne moved the ball from the Packers' 11-yard line to the New York 32 before being knocked out of bounds. His gain was three yards longer than what was awarded at the time.

In 1974, the stats crew at Metropolitan Stadium in Minnesota apparently forgot to count a carry for 10 yards by MacArthur Lane. Instead of six carries for 33 yards, he should have seven attempts for 43.

Those are three of the more glaring examples I have uncovered. There are more. One day I hope to list them all online.

What follows is a list of games from 1923 to the present for which I do not have complete play-by-plays:

Nov. 26, 1925	Nov. 22, 1936	Dec. 5, 1943
Nov. 28, 1925	Nov. 29, 1936	Oct. 29, 1944
Nov. 24, 1927	Nov. 21, 1937	Nov. 12, 1944
Nov. 29, 1928	Nov. 28, 1937	Dec. 1, 1946
Nov. 28, 1929	Nov. 12, 1939	Nov. 23, 1947
Nov. 27, 1930	Nov. 19, 1939	Dec. 14, 1947
Nov. 30, 1930		Nov. 7, 1948
Nov. 11, 1934	Most of 1941	Dec. 4, 1949
Nov. 25, 1934		Dec. 10, 1950
Nov. 29, 1934	Nov. 22, 1942	Oct. 28, 1951
Dec. 4, 1934	Nov. 29, 1942	Dec. 9, 1951
Nov. 8, 1936	Oct. 24, 1943	Dec. 14, 1952
Nov. 15, 1936	Oct. 31, 1943	Dec. 6, 1953

Acknowledgements

One never flies solo when producing a book. I am grateful for the help and kindness extended by the following individuals:

Cliff Christl hired me as a part-time sports reporter at the *Green Bay Press-Gazette* in 1986. He has answered countless Packers-related questions in the years since, and I continue to be amazed by his impeccable research and reporting in his role as the Packers' official team historian.

Tony Walter gave me an opportunity to write a numbers-based column about the team for the paper beginning in 1994. His belief in me only reinforced my desire to continue delving into statistical areas not yet explored.

Coach T.J. Troup and I have been exchanging information since his first phone call to me in late summer 2000. Friends now for nearly two decades, we continue to visit NFL Films, where we are often joined by fellow researchers John Maxymuk, John Richards, John Turney, Jeff Miller, Nick Webster and Chris Willis.

Most of the photographs in this book come courtesy of the *Green Bay Press-Gazette*. Obtaining them involved working with the paper as well as with the Khrome Agency, which had borrowed many of the negatives for its work in producing the 10-part documentary series entitled *Legacy: 100 Seasons of the Green Bay Packers*.

Robert Zizzo (regional sports editor for USA TODAY-NETWORK and *The Milwaukee Journal Sentinel*) graciously allowed the use of these photos, and he spent considerable time helping track down many of them. Julie Larson (sports planning editor for USA TODAY-NETWORK-Wisconsin) must have been a detective in an earlier life as she located a shot of Dorsey Levens and one of Mason Crosby after I had given up hope. (Thanks, Jeff Ash, for suggesting I contact Julie.)

Folks at the Khrome Agency were just as accommodating. Shelly Young (VP of video and animation), Amy Nitschke (video production coordinator), and Trevor Freiss (assistant producer) took valuable time away from their project and treated me as a special guest while I engaged in a search that took several days to complete.

Chip Manthey also contributed some of the wonderful photos you see here. Freelance photography is only one of Chip's many passions, and I am so thankful he is alive after experiencing a major health scare in December 2018. I wish you all the best, Chip, as you continue on your road to recovery!

Bob McGinn wrote the foreword to this book. I first met Bob in 1986 when he was the Packers beat reporter for the *Press-Gazette*. His interest in my statistical work got me thinking that my hobby might be more than just that.

I got to see Bob in action only a couple of times before he departed for *The Milwaukee Journal*, but that was enough to witness first-hand his pit bull determination. Many reporters travel in groups when approaching players in the locker room. Not Bob. He was on his own, gathering answers to questions regarding plays, formations, responsibilities and more; answers that supplied rich insight for his carefully crafted game accounts.

Finally, Mike Dauplaise and Bonnie Groessl of M&B Global Solutions Inc. partnered with me to produce this work. They served as editors, formatters, marketers and much more as we tasked ourselves with the goal of having copies ready before the start of the 2019 Packers season. We made it, and I greatly appreciate their efforts.

A number of online sites also aided my research:
- newspapers.com
- nflgsis.com
- pro-football-reference.com
- espn.com
- Google News Archives

Thank you, one and all, for the valuable help you provided. You helped make this journey fruitful and memorable.

Eric

The First Quarter

Eddie Lacy slashes for a first-quarter touchdown against the Atlanta Falcons at Lambeau Field in 2013. (Photo courtesy of the Green Bay Press-Gazette)

Longest First Plays

Yds.	Play	Date	Opponent
83	Don Hutson pass from Arnie Herber (TD)	Sept. 22, 1935	Bears
80	Antonio Freeman pass from Brett Favre (TD)	Nov. 1, 1998	49ers
79	James Lofton pass from Lynn Dickey (TD)	Oct. 21, 1984	Seahawks
78	Boyd Dowler pass from Bart Starr (TD)	Oct. 22, 1961	Vikings
77	Carroll Dale pass from Scott Hunter (TD)	Dec. 12, 1971	Bears
71	Gerry Ellis run	Dec. 4, 1983	Bears
62	Ryan Grant run (TD)	Dec. 13, 2009	Bears
60	Marquez Valdes-Scantling pass from Aaron Rodgers	Oct. 15, 2018	49ers

Leading Rushers on Opening Plays

Name	Att.	Yards	Avg.	LG	TD
Jim Taylor	48	263	5.48	21	0
Ahman Green	48	225	4.69	18	0
Ryan Grant	21	219	10.43	t62	2
Gerry Ellis	23	158	6.87	71	0
John Brockington	37	148	4.00	13	0

Leading Receivers on Opening Plays

Name	No.	Yards	Avg.	LG	TD
Donald Driver	14	118	8.43	17	0
Greg Jennings	8	55	6.89	10	0
Bill Schroeder	7	145	20.71	51	0
William Henderson	7	67	9.57	21	0
Gerry Ellis	7	7	1.00	11	0

Leading Passers on Opening Plays

Name	Att.	Com.	Yards	TD	HI
Brett Favre	121	76	835	1	2
Aaron Rodgers	72	53	430	0	0
Bart Starr	35	20	368	2	4
Lynn Dickey	39	24	215	1	2

First Impressions

Don Hutson

Don Hutson knew how to make a splash.

Hutson's first play against the Chicago Bears in 1935 was as compelling as any opening act. His long-distance excursion was the first clue that this spindly legged talent was on his way to redefining the end position.

Hutson scarcely mattered a week earlier in his first game as a pro. In brief stints against the Cardinals in the season opener, the rookie from Alabama downed a punt, assisted on a tackle, failed to gain on an end around, and had one pass thrown in his direction.

So, when Green Bay lined up for its first offensive play against the Bears, the opposition was focused on Johnny Blood. The veteran halfback was a far greater threat than any newcomer, or so Chicago believed.

Hutson split wide. At the snap, he dashed toward the center of the field, reached out and plucked a pass from the heavens. Without breaking stride, he hot-footed it for the end zone.

Photo courtesy of the Green Bay Press-Gazette

The catch-and-run, 83 yards in all, was the game's only touchdown. The Packers made it stand as they defeated their archrivals, 7-0.

"Many a Green Bay fan is moaning today because he was two minutes late yesterday afternoon," wrote John Walter of the *Green Bay Press-Gazette*. "Men who have witnessed hundreds of football games asserted unhesitatingly that the touchdown play which broke on the second play of the game (counting the kickoff) was the most spectacular effort they have ever seen on a gridiron.

"It took the experience of Arnold Herber (passer), the skill of Don Hutson (receiver) and the savage blocking of nine other Packers to execute it perfectly—timed to the split second.

"It was the play of the season."

Indeed. Though 10 games remained, nothing of such magnitude occurred during the weeks that followed. To this day, the Herber-to-Hutson connection remains the longest opening offensive play in Packers history.

That's remarkable. Green Bay has run more than 1,350 opening plays since its first league game against the Minneapolis Marines in 1921.

Some generated excitement. Some induced groans. The majority have long been forgotten.

The type and the distance covered can be determined for all but roughly 30 of these first salvos since 1923. Most gained fewer than 10 yards. Nine resulted in touchdowns.

Many players have been a party to these initial offerings. Some – Jim Taylor, John Brockington and Ahman Green – were called upon often. Others – Jim Jensen, Allen Rice and ReShard Lee – were one and done.

Hutson caught only one other opening-play pass. He traveled 21 yards with a pitch from Cecil Isbell in the 1941 regular-season finale.

That that play mattered little doesn't diminish Hutson. In the 11 seasons he suited up, Hutson more than lived up to the promise he displayed in 1935 when he introduced himself to the Bears and professional football.

Don Hutson (right) wields an oversized scissors to cut the ribbon at ceremonies dedicating the Packers' Don Hutson Center. Packers public relations director Lee Remmel looks on at left. (Photo courtesy of the Green Bay Press-Gazette)

November 12, 1967

Travis Williams welcomed the Cleveland Browns to Milwaukee County Stadium with a game-opening, 87-yard kickoff return for a touchdown in 1967. (Photo courtesy of the Green Bay Press-Gazette)

By the end of the first quarter, Nate Wallack may have regretted opening his mouth.

Wallack, Cleveland's publicity director, provided an optimistic assessment of his Century Division-leading Browns (5-3) prior to their matchup with the Packers (5-2-1) on November 12, 1967.

"Our team has started to jell a bit. In fact, some people feel we shouldn't have lost a game. We've been ahead in every game we lost."

Wallack then listed the scores by which the Browns had led in each of their losses. As those in his line of work are wont to do, Wallack accentuated the positive.

"If you look at the points allowed, you will see that we're among the lowest in the league."

Remaining upbeat was about to become nigh near impossible.

Travis Williams returned the opening kickoff for a touchdown in that 1967 meeting between the Packers and Browns. Marv Fleming caught a scoring pass from Bart Starr. Donny Anderson chipped in not one, but two touchdowns: the first on a plunge and the second on a pass reception.

In short order, Green Bay was up 28-0. But the Packers weren't done.

Williams was afforded a second chance at a return after Ernie Green scored for Cleveland. The Road Runner flashed 85 yards for a fifth Packer TD.

"I've never seen things go your way so much so early in the game," Starr said in reference to the 35 points. "Those kickoff returns were a thing of beauty."

Green Bay's takeover of the end zone set an NFL record for first-quarter points. The outpouring was too much for the Browns, who succumbed 55-7.

Though shell shocked, Cleveland recovered sufficiently to made the playoffs. It did not, however, come close to allowing the fewest points in the league.

The First Quarter

Though it may appear to be just another 15-minute segment of the game, the first quarter is different.

It is the only one in which opponents are guaranteed to start on equal terms. Game plans are unveiled. What works and what doesn't soon becomes apparent.

Mistakes will be made. But, unlike later in the game, ample time remains for remedy.

Sometimes first quarters foreshadow action to come. What transpires early can provide insight into whether the game will be a defensive struggle, a shootout, or a blowout.

Green Bay's opening against the Browns remains one of its finest. The team has had other memorable first quarters.

> **October 25, 1931**—Weert Engelmann became the only Packer to score three touchdowns in the first quarter. He counted on passes of 29 and 32 yards, and returned a kickoff for a score as Green Bay flattened the Providence Steam Roller 48-20.
>
> **September 26, 2004**—Brett Favre and Indianapolis Colts quarterback Peyton Manning engaged in a mind-numbing exhibition of marksmanship. In the game's first 11 minutes, the two went back and forth completing 17 of 22 passes for 336 yards and five touchdowns (158.1 rating). Indianapolis came out on top, 45-31.
>
> **September 8, 2011**—Aaron Rodgers connected on 14 of 15 throws for 188 yards. He fired three touchdown passes – a team record for a first quarter – as Green Bay turned back the New Orleans Saints 42-34.

1st Quarter Rushing

Jim Taylor
1958 - 1966

Jim Taylor is stopped by Detroit Lions middle linebacker Joe Schmidt on Green Bay's opening drive on November 8, 1964. Later in the quarter, Taylor ripped off an 84-yard run, the longest of his career. (Photo courtesy of the Green Bay Press-Gazette)

Would Jim Taylor have made the longest run of his professional career against the Detroit Lions had Joe Schmidt been on the field?

We'll never know.

Taylor, a Hall of Fame running back, made history in the second meeting between the Packers and Lions in 1964.

Schmidt, a Hall of Fame linebacker, saw his season come to an abrupt end.

Fog surrounded City Stadium when Green Bay and Detroit met on that second Sunday of November. What soon became clear: the Packers were the better team.

Green Bay rolled up 434 yards, including 232 on the ground, in downing Detroit 30-7. The team scored on each of its first three possessions and only surrendered a meaningless touchdown with nine seconds to play.

Taylor made an impact from the start. He carried eight times for 105 yards and two scores in the opening 15 minutes to become the first Packer to rush for 100 or more yards in a first quarter.

The human battering ram picked up 19 yards on six tries during Green Bay's initial, 12-play march. He plowed in from a yard out on his sixth attempt to put the Packers ahead 7-0.

By then, Schmidt was out. The perennial All-Pro had suffered a dislocated shoulder two plays earlier while attempting to tackle Bart Starr as the quarterback skipped ahead for 14 yards and a first down.

Taylor's seventh carry went the distance. The fullback accepted a handoff from Starr and powered 84 yards to the end zone.

Unlike many runs of that length, it was not an unimpeded sprint. Taylor had to battle to reach pay dirt.

"I could feel somebody coming up on me toward the end," Taylor said. "(Bob) Skoronski had (Dick) LeBeau going in front of me, but I figured I couldn't break out past LeBeau. So I decided to just stay in there behind Bob."

LeBeau wasn't the only Lion breathing down Taylor's neck. Linebacker Wayne Walker joined the scrum.

"Then I felt a little more load on my back than I figured on – that was Walker getting into it," Taylor continued. "But I was driving for that flag. I made up my mind they weren't going to get me out of bounds before I got into the end zone."

Forrest Gregg and Boyd Dowler made key blocks to help spring the determined fullback.

Taylor got one more opportunity in the quarter. He advanced two yards to reach 105 for the quarter before Paul Hornung closed the period with an 8-yard gain.

Taylor was the team's primary land rover during most of Vince Lombardi's time as coach of the Packers (1959-67). He rushed for more than 1,000 yards in five consecutive seasons (1960-64).

The fullback also rushed for more than 300 yards in the first quarter in each of those five seasons. That's a team record.

Taylor is the Packers' all-time first-quarter rushing leader. In nine seasons (1958-66) he piled up 2,233 yards on 506 attempts (4.41 average).

His best season was 1961. That year he amassed 426 yards on 72 trips (5.92) and scored four rushing touchdowns.

Taylor carried at least once in 55 straight first quarters (1960-64). The streak came to an end when he sat out a 24-23 loss to the Vikings with a shoulder injury.

Taylor finished with 145 yards rushing on that foggy afternoon against the Lions. A frustrated Schmidt contemplated retirement, but returned for one final go-round in 1965.

First-Quarter Rushing

Career
Packers who rushed for more than 1,000 yards in the first quarter.

Yards	Player	Att.	Avg.	LG	TD
2,233	Jim Taylor	506	4.41	t84	11
2,129	Ahman Green	524	4.06	83	13
1,337	Ryan Grant	275	4.86	t62	11
1,187	Eddie Lacy	245	4.84	44	6
1,165	John Brockington	337	3.46	41	5
1,097	Paul Hornung	293	3.74	54	13

Season
Packers who rushed for more than 375 first-quarter yards in a season.

Yards	Player, Year	Att.	Avg.	LG	TD
550	Ahman Green, 2003	107	5.14	t65	5
476	Eddie Lacy, 2014	78	6.10	44	4
426	Jim Taylor, 1961	72	5.92	45	4
417	Ahman Green, 2001	82	5.09	t83	4
378	Ryan Grant, 2009	88	4.30	t62	5

Game
Packers who rushed for more than 80 yards in the first quarter of a game.

Yards	Player, Date	Att.	Avg.	LG	TD
122	Ahman Green, Sept. 9, 2001	4	30.50	t83	2
105	Jim Taylor, Nov. 8, 1964	8	13.13	t84	2
96	Aaron Jones, Nov. 11, 2018	4	24.00	67	0
95	Ahman Green, Sept. 14, 2003	9	10.56	t65	1
91	James Starks, Oct. 18, 2015	3	30.33	t65	1
85	Ryan Grant, Dec. 13, 2009	7	12.14	t62	1
81	Ryan Grant, Nov. 11, 2007	8	10.13	t30	1
81	DeShawn Wynn, Dec. 28, 2008	2	40.50	t73	1

Eric Goska

First-Quarter Receiving

Career
Packers who caught 100 or more first-quarter passes.

No.	Player	Yards	Avg.	LG	TD
156	Donald Driver	2,109	13.52	t85	10
135	Jordy Nelson	2,126	15.75	t80	17
126	Sterling Sharpe	1,542	12.24	t65	13
125	Randall Cobb	1,356	10.85	t70	11
119	James Lofton	2,135	17.94	t79	13
*108	Don Hutson	1,897	17.56	t92	22
100	Boyd Dowler	1,651	16.51	t78	10

*Hutson's career numbers (excluding TDs) are incomplete.

Season
Packers who caught 24 or more first-quarter passes in a season.

No.	Player, Year	Yards	Avg.	LG	TD
33	Jordy Nelson, 2014	507	15.36	t66	3
31	Sterling Sharpe, 1993	324	10.45	t50	4
28	Robert Brooks, 1995	349	12.46	30	3
26	Jordy Nelson, 2016	409	15.73	58	6
24	James Lofton, 1981	453	18.88	t75	2
24	Donald Driver, 2006	298	12.42	48	1

Game
Packers who caught five or more first-quarter passes in a game.

No.	Player, Date	Yards	Avg.	LG	TD
6	John Jefferson, Nov. 6, 1983	92	15.33	28	1
6	Sterling Sharpe, Oct. 10, 1993	35	5.83	11	0
6	Greg Jennings, Sept. 25, 2011	78	13.00	19	0
5	Don Hutson, Nov. 23, 1941	51	10.20	13	0
5	Sterling Sharpe, Nov. 18, 1990	98	19.60	t54	1
5	Davante Adams, Nov. 15, 2015	37	7.40	18	0
5	Randall Cobb, Oct. 9, 2016	53	10.60	17	0
5	Randall Cobb, Dec. 10, 2017	29	5.80	16	0

1st Quarter Receiving

James Lofton
1978 - 1986

James Lofton's one-handed catch earned him a second first-quarter touchdown against the Seattle Seahawks on October 21, 1984. (Photo courtesy of the Green Bay Press-Gazette)

James Lofton's time in the 20-yard dash is unknown.

Before he was a receiver for the Packers, Lofton was an outstanding track and field athlete at Stanford University. He ran 100 meters in 10.3 seconds, 200 meters in 20.5 seconds, and 400 meters in 46.4 seconds.

Lofton was no stranger to a stopwatch.

The long strider also finished first in the long jump at the 1978 NCAA Outdoor Track and Field Championships with a leap of 26-feet-11¾. The distance exceeded the NCAA record of 26-11, but was not recognized because it was wind-aided.

Speed and distance: Lofton was big on both in his NFL career.

The Packers selected Lofton sixth overall in the 1978 draft. He is the only receiver from that class to have been inducted into the Pro Football Hall of Fame.

James Lofton celebrates after catching his then-Packers record 489th reception in an October 5, 1986, game against the Cincinnati Bengals at Milwaukee County Stadium. (Photo courtesy of the Green Bay Press-Gazette)

"Most of the time people think of a track athlete as somebody they send deep and hope he holds onto the ball," Lofton said shortly after being drafted. "I wouldn't put myself in that category."

Lofton did go deep…and he usually held onto the ball.

For nine seasons (1978-86), Lofton was the Packers' big-play specialist. He caught 530 passes for 9,656 yards. Both were team records at the time.

An impressive 187 of Lofton's receptions – more than a third of everything he caught – stretched for 20 or more yards. He was 20/20 six times; that is, he caught 20 or more passes for 20 or more yards in 1979 (20), 1980 (28), 1981 (23), 1983 (22), 1984 (29) and 1985 (24).

In 1983, Lofton led the NFL with an average of 22.4 yards per reception. He was again No. 1 in 1984 with a mark of 22.0.

When getting to 20, Lofton seemingly always had a good time.

Mel Blount was a believer. The Pittsburgh Steelers' defensive back covered Lofton in the second game of the 1983 season. That day, Lofton caught five passes for 169 yards and three touchdowns, including scores of 71 and 73 yards.

"One-on-one it would be very difficult to cover him (Lofton)," Blount said. "If anybody has the ability to do it, it's me. And I didn't get it done."

Lofton's tendency to go long showed up in the first quarter as well. There he seized 119 passes for a team-record 2,135 yards and 13 touchdowns.

More than a third (43) of his first-quarter catches went for 20 yards or more. He had at least two first-quarter 20-yarders every season in Green Bay, with a career-best nine in 1985.

Those early, long catches often paid off. Forty resulted in first downs. Thirty-one spurred drives that led to points.

Lofton led or shared the team lead in first-quarter receptions six times. He was most productive in 1981, when he corralled 24 for 453 yards and two touchdowns.

Lofton caught at least one first-quarter pass in 78 of 136 games as a Packer. In 40 of those games, he had at least one that covered 20 or more yards.

Sadly, Lofton's big-play potential waned in his final season in Green Bay. Head coach Forrest Gregg adopted a ball-control offense that kept No. 80 closer to the line of scrimmage.

Lofton hauled in just eight first-quarter passes in 1986, and only two gained 20 or more yards.

Twenty Aplenty

Players who caught the most passes of 20 or more yards in their Packers career.

Player, Years	No.	Yards	Avg.	LG	TD
James Lofton, 1978-1986	187	5,674	30.34	t80	27
Donald Driver, 1999-2012	143	4,679	32.72	t85	32
Don Hutson, 1935-1945	115	4,379	38.08	t92	52
Max McGee, 1954, 1957-1967	108	3,698	34.24	t82	36
Sterling Sharpe, 1988-1994	107	3,416	31.93	t79	28
Jordy Nelson, 2008-2014, 2016-2017	106	3,827	36.10	t93	28
Greg Jennings, 2007-2012	97	3,521	36.30	t86	27
Boyd Dowler, 1959-1969	94	2,990	31.81	t91	19
Antonio Freeman, 1995-2001, 2003	89	2,982	33.51	t84	26
Carroll Dale, 1965-1972	87	3,178	36.53	t89	24
James Jones, 2007-2013, 2015	79	2,736	34.63	t83	21
Randall Cobb, 2011-2018	79	2,355	29.81	t75	15
Bill Howton, 1952-1958	76	3,102	40.82	t90	26

First-Quarter Passing

Career
Packers who threw for 2,000 or more first-quarter yards in their career.

Name	Att	Com	Yds	TD	HI	Rate
Brett Favre	1,892	1,173	13,614	93	49	89.32
Aaron Rodgers	1,275	845	10,144	81	12	107.72
Bart Starr	796	454	6,427	36	38	78.44
Lynn Dickey	631	357	4,831	30	27	79.15
Tobin Rote*	401	169	2,324	16	22	53.06
Don Majkowski	284	156	2,093	10	8	78.57

Rote's totals (excluding TD passes) are higher. There are five games for which complete information does not exist.

Season
Packers who threw for 1,000 or more first-quarter yards in a season.

Name, Season	Att	Com	Yds	TD	HI	Rate
Aaron Rodgers, 2014	143	97	1,388	10	0	122.36
Aaron Rodgers, 2009	141	90	1,258	7	2	103.08
Lynn Dickey, 1983	111	71	1,160	7	3	108.69
Brett Favre, 1995	144	98	1,149	10	6	97.83
Aaron Rodgers, 2011	121	89	1,094	11	0	131.35
Aaron Rodgers, 2016	143	96	1,083	10	1	109.98
Aaron Rodgers, 2010	112	73	1,072	6	3	102.98
Brett Favre, 1998	130	80	1,041	10	4	99.55

Game
Packers who threw for 150 or more first-quarter yards in a game.

Name, Date	Att	Com	Yds	TD	HI	Rate
Aaron Rodgers, Oct. 26, 2014	9	7	203	1	0	155.79
Aaron Rodgers, Sept. 8, 2011	15	14	188	3	0	158.33
Brett Favre, Oct. 7, 2002	11	8	180	2	0	154.36
Aaron Rodgers, Oct. 15, 2018	9	6	170	1	0	146.76
Aaron Rodgers, Oct. 24, 2010	7	6	166	0	1	79.17
Lynn Dickey, Oct. 21, 1984	10	8	164	2	0	158.33
Aaron Rodgers, Dec. 24, 2016	13	12	163	2	0	158.33
Aaron Rodgers, Nov. 16, 2014	14	9	158	1	0	126.49
Don Majkowski, Oct. 25, 1987	10	7	155	1	0	145.83
Lynn Dickey, Oct. 2, 1983	8	5	151	1	0	145.83
Bart Starr, Sept. 27, 1970	6	6	151	1	0	158.33

1st Quarter Passing

Aaron Rodgers
2005 - 2018

Aaron Rodgers, shown here throwing against the Tennessee Titans in 2012, is the Packers' highest-rated quarterback in first-quarter play. (Photo courtesy of the Green Bay Press-Gazette)

Aaron Rodgers is all about ratings.

If he were a bond, he'd be triple A. If he were a hotel, he'd be 5-star.

The quarterback from California is upper echelon regardless of what system is used to grade his performance. He's the highest-rated passer in NFL history, one of only two (Russell Wilson) to have a career rating (103.8) in triple digits (minimum 1,500 attempts).

Since becoming a starter in 2008, Rodgers has earned a passer rating greater than 100 in an NFL-record seven seasons. His run of six straight (2009-14) is also a league record.

In 2011, Rodgers set the single-season mark at 122.5.

"You want to be recognized for your play, being consistent, being a guy your teammates can count on," Rodgers said after receiving the NFL's Most Valuable Player award following the team's 15-1 run in 2011.

Rodgers has excelled in the first quarter. His rating there (107.7) is better than his marks in the second (101.8), third (101.6) and fourth quarters (103.3).

Interestingly, Rodgers did not attempt a first-quarter pass in any of his first three seasons. It was only after he no longer backed up Brett Favre that he got a chance to test his arm early.

The efficient quarterback has enjoyed seven seasons with a first-quarter rating above 100 (2009-14, 2016). He exceeded 100 in 2017, but did not have enough attempts to qualify, having missed nine games due to a collarbone injury.

His first-quarter mark of 131.4 in 2011 is a franchise best.

One reason Rodgers rates highly is his aversion to interceptions. He's thrown just 12 in the first quarter despite having attempted 1,275 passes there.

Not one of Rodgers' initial 107 first-quarter attempts was picked off. Alex Brown of the Chicago Bears ended that streak on December 22, 2008.

Since that time, Rodgers has fashioned five additional first-quarter streaks

Aaron Rodgers (12) and former teammate Charles Woodson meet following the Packers' 30-20 victory over the Raiders in Oakland in 2015. (Photo courtesy of the Green Bay Press-Gazette)

of more than 100 attempts without an interception. His longest – 225 straight – stretched from mid-December 2010 to late November 2012. He entered the 2019 season having thrown his last 156 first-quarter passes without an interception.

While interceptions have been scarce, yards have come in bunches. Rodgers has thrown for more than 1,000 first-quarter yards in five different seasons. Favre (twice) and Lynn Dickey (once) are the only other Packers to have surpassed 1,000.

Touchdowns, too, show up often. Rodgers' 81 first-quarter scoring passes are second to the 93 of Favre, but Rodgers' TD percentage (6.35 percent) is unmatched.

The Packers have been unbeatable when Rodgers throws multiple touchdown passes in the opening 15 minutes. The two-time league MVP has done it 10 times, and Green Bay is 10-0 in those games.

Never was Rodgers more ready than against the New Orleans Saints in 2011. He dazzled on a 68-degree Thursday night as the NFL kicked off its 92nd season in Green Bay.

Rodgers completed 14 of 15 passes for 188 yards. He hurled scoring passes to receivers Greg Jennings, Jordy Nelson and Randall Cobb.

Three times did the Packers have the ball. Three times did they score.

Not a sack, nor a less-than-perfect snap, nor a pair of penalties could stop Rodgers. He completed his first seven passes, threw one away when pressured by defensive end Jeff Charleston, then completed seven more.

A sack by linebacker Jonathan Casillas threatened to derail the Packers' first advance. But Rodgers fielded center Scott Wells' next snap – low and outside – and fired to Donald Driver to erase third-and-12. Four plays later, Rodgers placed the ball on Jennings' back shoulder from seven yards out and Green Bay led 7-0.

Guard T.J. Lang's false start put the Packers in second-and-goal from the Saints' 11-yard line the next time out. Undeterred, Rodgers located Driver for eight before tossing a 3-yarder to Nelson in the south end zone. Green Bay led 14-0.

A second false start penalty on Lang created first-and-15 on Green Bay's third possession. Passes to Cobb and Jennings gained 13, and Rodgers then pitched to tight end Jermichael Finley for 18 and a first down at the Saints' 32.

On the Packers' final play of the quarter, Rodgers flipped to Cobb who, after eluding defensive back Malcolm Jenkins, raised the ball into the air and launched himself into the end zone. Mason Crosby's point after sent the Packers ahead 21-7.

With that, Rodgers had become the first Packer to throw three touchdowns in the first quarter of a game.

"It (the great start) doesn't surprise me at all out of him," Jennings said. "He's very poised, and especially when the lights are turned on, he comes to play. The lights were definitely turned on bright, and we stepped up and came away with the win (42-34) today."

Rodgers didn't throw another TD pass that night. But his early work forced New Orleans to play catchup, and it never got closer than four despite three TD passes from Drew Brees.

As for ratings, Rodgers couldn't have started the season any better. He earned a passer rating of 158.3 in that first quarter, the maximum allowed in the National Football League.

First-Quarter Scoring

Career
Packers who scored 150 or more points in the first quarter.

Points	Name	TDs	PAT	FG
286	Mason Crosby	0	139-141	49-65
190	Ryan Longwell	0	76-79	38-45
183	Paul Hornung	16	42-43	15-36
175	Chris Jacke	0	64-64	37-43
173	Don Hutson	22	41-44	0-3

Season
Packers who scored more than 30 points in the first quarter of one season.

Points	Name, Season	TDs	PAT	FG
39	Paul Hornung, 1961	3	12-12	3-3
37	Mason Crosby, 2009	0	13-13	8-11
37	Mason Crosby, 2014	0	19-19	6-6
36	Jordy Nelson, 2016	6	0-0	0-0
34	Chris Jacke, 1996	0	7-7	9-9
32	Chester Marcol, 1972	0	8-8	8-12

Game
Packers who scored more than 12 points in the first quarter of a game.

Points	Name, Date	TDs	PAT	FG
18	Wuert Engelmann, Oct. 25, 1931	3	0-0	0-0
17	Paul Hornung, Nov. 26, 1959	2	2-2	1-1
14	Paul Hornung, Sept. 16, 1962	2	2-2	0-0

1st Quarter Scoring

Weert Engelmann
1930 - 1933

Speed was Weert Engelmann's forte. It served him well in basketball, football and track.

It was no surprise, then, that Engelmann wasted little time when crafting his signature moment in Packers history.

The Packers won their first NFL championship in 1929. Green Bay (12-0-1) finished ahead of the New York Giants (13-1-1) – a team it defeated 20-6 in New York in November – to claim top honors in the league.

On a cold night in early December, an estimated 20,000 fans surrounded the Northwestern Railroad Station in Green Bay to greet the team when it arrived after clinching the title with a 25-0 victory over the Chicago Bears. Each Packers player received a warm welcome as he got off the train.

There was little chance the Packers would become complacent after reaching the top. Head coach Curly Lambeau was always on the lookout for new talent and discovered Engelmann in 1930.

Weert Engelmann, taken from the 1931 team photo (Eric Goska collection)

Engelmann had led South Dakota State to three consecutive NCIC track championships, and that year he won the discus event at the Drake Relays with a toss of 154 feet, 6 inches.

Two years earlier, Engelmann had come tantalizingly close to representing the United States in the Olympics. Tryouts for the decathlon were held at Franklin Field in Philadelphia, and Engelmann had come within a quarter of a point of making the four-man team, finishing fifth out of a field of 35.

Twenty-five years later, he recounted the near miss.

"The pole broke just as I was pulling up to go over the bar and I hit the edge of the pit with my shoulder as I came down," Engelmann told *Green Bay Press-Gazette* sports reporter Lee Remmel. "The javelin (one of his better events) came after that. A throw of 165 feet would have put me in. But with the shoulder in that condition, the best I could do was 135 feet."

In the interview, Engelmann also recalled his most memorable game with the Packers. His favorite was a 48-20 win over the Providence Steam Roller in 1931.

"I scored three touchdowns in the first six minutes," he said.

Engelmann's 18-point first quarter is a team record. It is the quickest Green Bay has scored its initial three TDs in any game.

"Engelmann scampers alone across the goal line," read the heading above the photo in the *Green Bay Press-Gazette* the day after. No other player was visible in the shot that captured Engelmann's No. 25 jersey moving away from the camera.

The back caught two TD passes from Red Dunn. The first, a 29-yarder, capped Green Bay's first drive. The second, from 32 yards out, ended the team's third offensive series.

Perhaps reeling from those two quick scores, Providence made a move it would regret. It chose to kick off.

In those days, the scored-upon team often sent the ball back to the scoring team in hopes of pinning them deep and perhaps forcing a turnover. This thinking might have been sound had anyone but Engelmann been back to receive the boot.

Lew Pope kicked and the ball landed in the mitts of the hottest man on the field. Engelmann headed toward the south side of the field, weaved through traffic at midfield, and then breezed past the last remaining defender, who was rendered irrelevant by a block from Elmer Sleight at the Steam Roller 10.

Engelmann had zipped 80 yards to a third touchdown. The kickoff return for a touchdown was the first in Packers history.

With nine minutes remaining in the opening quarter, Green Bay led 21-0. Engelmann had wheeled to 145 all-purpose yards; Providence had 19.

That windfall helped make the 1931 season Engelmann's most productive. He rushed 41 times for 261 yards (6.37 average) and caught nine passes for 203 yards.

At season's end, Green Bay claimed a third straight NFL championship. The team hadn't rested on its laurels, and the halfback from South Dakota had proven to be a solid addition.

The *Press-Gazette* took note of Engelmann's speed in August 1933.

"One of the fastest backs on the 1932 Packer professional football squad, Wuert Engelmann, has signed his contract for the coming season Coach E. L. Lambeau announced today."

Engelmann scored 10 touchdowns in his career. Six arrived in the first quarter.

He scored his last on October 29, 1933, against the Philadelphia Eagles. He waylaid a Swede Hanson pass and returned it 55 yards to put Green Bay ahead 14-0 en route to a 35-9 victory.

In attendance that day was Engelmann's father. The older gentleman had immigrated to the United States from Germany at the age of 14. He was interviewed during the week leading to the game and was happy to set the record straight regarding his son's first name.

"I guess they made a mistake right at the start and never changed it," he said of his son's first name which often appeared in print as Wuert. "The boy's name is the same as mine, which in Low German is Weert."

Weert senior headed back to South Dakota after the victory. Weert junior missed the next two games with injuries to his arm and shoulder.

When Engelmann returned to action, his workload was greatly reduced. He was released after the game of November 26, 1933, with the Giants.

Decades later, Engelmann was inducted into three different South Dakota halls of fame. He had lived up to the nickname of his college – the Jackrabbits.

Green Bay Packers vs. Providence Steam Roller
October 25, 1931, at City Stadium (*Green Bay Press-Gazette* play-by-play)

Note: In this era, the scored-upon team often kicked the ball back to the scoring team in hopes of pinning them deep and perhaps forcing a turnover.

GB's Mike Michalske kicks off to Pop Williams returns +20
[Providence possession]
1-10-P29   Pop Williams runs FUMBLE, recovered by GB's Elmer Sleight

[Green Bay possession]
1-10-P24   Weert Engelmann runs +6
2-4-P18   PENALTY GB offside +5
2-9-P23   Weert Engelmann runs -2
3-11-P25   Herdis McCrary runs -4
4-15-P29   Red Dunn pass ***Weert Engelmann +29 TOUCHDOWN***, Dunn kicks

Lew Pope (Providence) kicks off to GB's Tom Nash returns +20
[Green Bay possession]
1-10-G46   Herdis McCrary runs +0
2-10-G46   Hank Bruder runs +5
3-5-P49   Hank Bruder runs -2 (Al Graham tackles)
4-7-G49   Hank Bruder punts +51 into the end zone for touchback

[Providence possession]
1-10-P20   Pop Williams runs +0 (Hank Bruder tackles)
2-10-P20   Lew Pope runs -1
3-11-P19   Pop Williams punts +17 dead on P36

[Green Bay possession]
1-10-P36   Herdis McCrary runs +6
2-4-P30   Hank Bruder runs +3
3-1-P27   PENALTY GB offside +5
3-6-P32   Red Dunn pass ***Weert Englemann +32 TOUCHDOWN***, Dunn kicks

Lew Pope (Providence) kicks off to GB's ***Weert Englemann returns +80 TOUCHDOWN***, Dunn kicks

The Second Quarter

End Don Hutson (left) and halfback Cecil Isbell talk with Packers coach Curly Lambeau in this 1941 publicity photo taken at City Stadium. (Photo courtesy of the Green Bay Press-Gazette)

November 9, 2014

Jordy Nelson heads downfield during the Packers' 55-14 victory over the Chicago Bears at Lambeau Field. (Photo courtesy of the Green Bay Press-Gazette)

On this particular day, the Packers weren't merely poking the Bear. They were prodding, pushing and pounding the beast.

What took place on November 9, 2014, was either highly entertaining or highly depressing, depending on your point of view. Green Bay manhandled Chicago 55-14 in a game that was essentially over by halftime.

The Packers scored touchdowns on each of their first five drives. They pounced so quickly and so decisively that starting quarterback Aaron Rodgers went to the bench early in the third quarter.

The Green and Gold was downright ruthless in the second quarter. The team scored 28 points in using less than six minutes of game clock.

Chicago trailed 42-0 at halftime, having surrendered a franchise-record for first-half points.

Green Bay was offensively gifted in 2014. It ranked first in points scored (486) and sixth in yards gained (6,178).

The club specialized in first-half acquisition. In the opening 30 minutes, it was No. 1 in points (310), yards (3,690), passing yards (2,658), first downs (212), passing first downs (135), average gain per play (6.86), and average gain per passing play (8.10).

Rodgers kept the juggernaut humming. In fashioning an NFL-best first-half rating of 120.3, Rodgers fired 25 touchdowns and no interceptions.

Jordy Nelson (nine) and Randall Cobb (seven) caught the majority of those first-half scoring passes. Davante Adams (two), Eddie Lacy (two), Andrew Quarless (two), Richard Rodgers (two) and Brandon Bostick (one) nabbed the others.

Green Bay was unbeatable at Lambeau Field. In going 8-0, the Green and Gold scored 212 first-half points, an NFL record. Rodgers's 19 touchdown passes accounted for much of that total.

Rodgers and the offense scored on 32 of 45 first-half possessions (71.1 percent) at the fabled field in 2014, converting 32 of 50 first downs.

With all this production, it's hard to believe that in early September, Rodgers felt compelled to relay this message on his radio show out of Milwaukee:

"Five letters here, just for everybody out there in Packerland: R-E-L-A-X. We're going to be fine."

That admonishment came on the heels of a 19-7 loss in Detroit that dropped Green Bay to 1-2. But by the time the Bears (3-5) came calling, the Packers (5-3) were headed in the right direction.

Rarely has a quarterback opened as forcefully as Rodgers did in the deconstruction of Chicago. He completed 18 of 24 passes for 315 yards and six touchdowns – all in the first half.

He and his receiving corps let loose in the second quarter. In no time, the Packers' side of the scoreboard went from 14 to 42.

Rodgers connected with Nelson for a 73-yard touchdown. The play took 12 seconds.

The duo struck again, this time from 40 yards out. Ninety seconds came off the clock during that four-play, 54-yard advance.

The team took its time (three minutes, 10 seconds) on its next outing, in part because it had to travel 95 yards. Lacy cashed in on a 56-yard reception as Green Bay went up 35-0.

Cobb finally brought an end to the onslaught. His 18-yard reception ended a six-play, 48-second affair that put the game out of reach.

Bears quarterback Jay Cutler kneeled to end the half. He should have waved a white flag.

Green Bay ran 18 plays and gained 265 yards in scoring 28 points in the second quarter. The yardage was a Packers record for a quarter.

Rodgers had as many touchdown passes (four) as he did incompletions in the period. His 242 passing yards are the most by any Packers passer in a quarter.

Many marveled at the apparent ease with which Green Bay's offense operated in 2014. Rodgers made clear that what might have appeared routine was anything but.

"It's not easy to do this every week. We put a lot of time in. We all do. We prepare to be successful." he explained.

In the second quarter against the Bears, Nelson snagged four passes for 133 yards and two scores. His was the third-most productive second quarter in team annals, behind the 168 of Bill Howton in 1956 and the 144 of Don Hutson in 1945.

Cobb caught three for 51 yards in the same 15-minute span. His touchdown reception made up for a fumble he lost on the previous drive.

"That was one of the top performances since I've been here offensively," Cobb said. "We put things together so well and were able to make the plays. It was really a great game."

The Second Quarter

It is the final period of the first half. It's all hands on deck as combatants jockey to either produce or prevent one last score before halftime. Teams are intent upon heading into intermission on a positive note. Each seeks to put itself in the best position possible ahead of the second half.

Green Bay's mauling of the Bears remains one of its finest second quarters. There have been others.

> **October 7, 1945**—The Packers scored 41 points in a 57-21 romp over the Detroit Lions at State Fair Park in West Allis. Don Hutson caught six passes for 144 yards and four touchdowns, while Roy McKay completed 7 of 11 passes for 199 yards and four scores. Hutson tallied an NFL-record 29 points in the period.
>
> **October 21, 1956**—Bill Howton snagged five passes for 168 yards and a touchdown as Green Bay defeated the Rams 42-17 at Milwaukee County Stadium. In the order he made them, Howton's catches measured 36, 14, 11, 63 (touchdown) and 44 yards.
>
> **December 20, 1992**—Green Bay scored four touchdowns within seven minutes to knock off the Rams 28-13 at Lambeau Field. The win, the Packers' sixth in a row and its longest streak since opening the 1965 season with six straight victories, ensured the team had a winning record in Mike Holmgren's first season as head coach.

Second-Quarter Rushing

Career
Packers who rushed for more than 1,000 yards in the second quarter.

Yards	Player	Att.	Avg.	LG	TD
2,158	Ahman Green	488	4.42	38	15
2,099	Jim Taylor	465	4.51	53	22
1,614	John Brockington	348	4.64	53	12
1,060	Ryan Grant	241	4.40	t66	9

Season
Packers who rushed for more than 350 second-quarter yards in a season.

Yards	Player, Year	Att.	Avg.	LG	TD
454	John Brockington, 1973	80	5.68	53	0
429	Ahman Green, 2003	95	4.52	24	2
409	Ahman Green, 2002	81	5.05	38	3
375	John Brockington, 1971	54	6.94	52	2
358	John Brockington, 1972	78	4.59	30	4

Game
Packers who rushed for more than 70 yards in the second quarter of a game.

Yards	Player, Date	Att.	Avg.	LG	TD
95	Ty Montgomery, Dec. 18, 2016	3	31.67	61	0
88	Samkon Gado, Dec. 11, 2005	7	12.57	t64	1
81	Ryan Grant, Oct. 29, 2007	14	5.79	24	0
78	John Brockington, Nov. 7, 1971	10	7.80	22	1
74	Lew Carpenter, Oct. 25, 1959	4	18.50	t55	1
73	Ryan Grant, Dec. 23, 2007	6	12.17	t66	1
72	Donny Anderson, Sept. 24, 1967	6	12.00	40	0

2nd Quarter Rushing

John Brockington
1971 - 1977

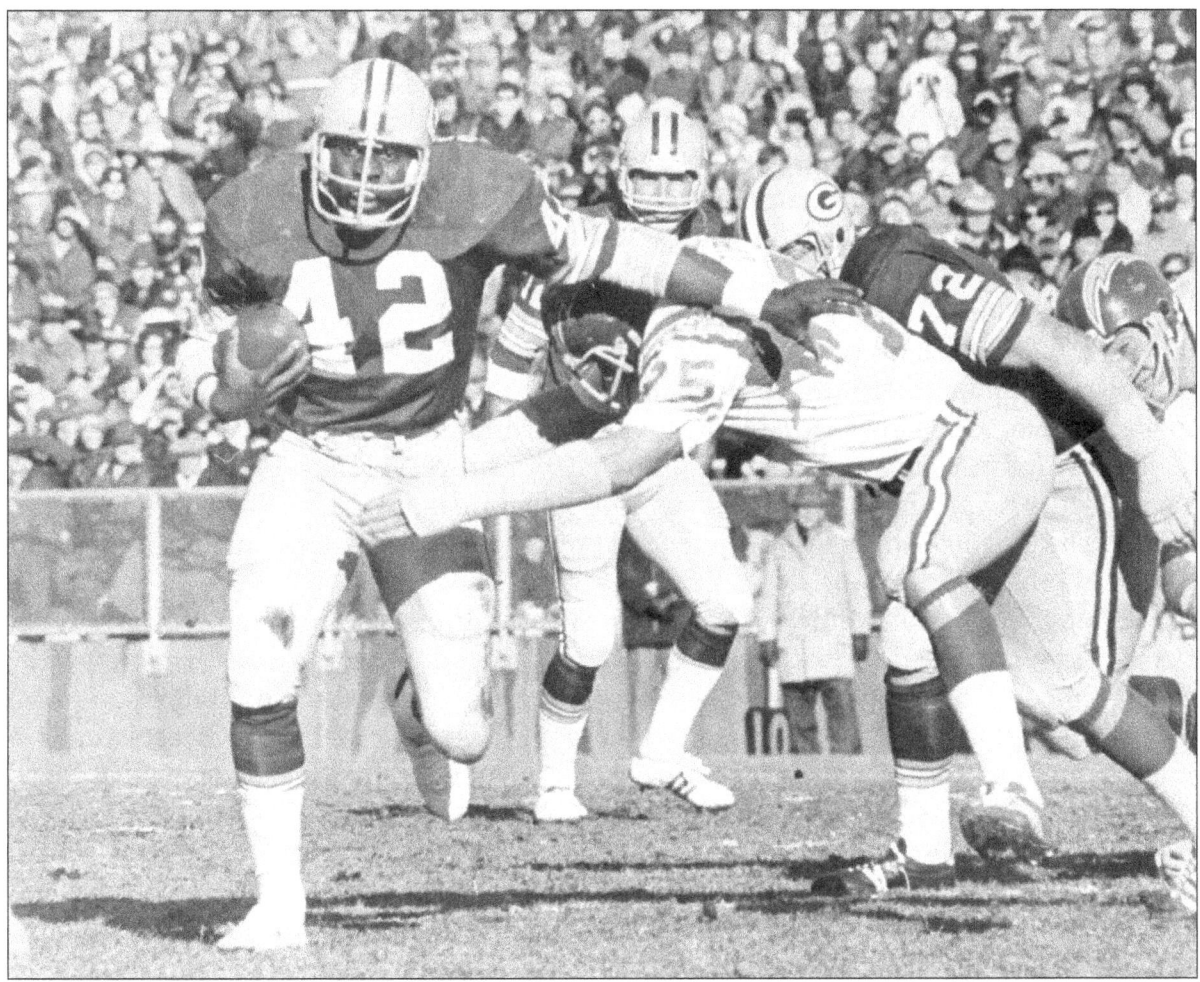

John Brockington became the first Packers running back to gain 1,000 yards rushing as a rookie. Here he makes a gain against the San Diego Chargers in 1974, his fourth season in the league. (Photo courtesy of the Green Bay Press-Gazette)

John Brockington injected a new hue into the Black and Blue Division. Call it deep purple.

The Green Bay Packers' first-round draft choice in 1971 was a brawler. A punishing runner, Brockington left more than one defender bruised and contused.

Brockington became just the fourth player in NFL history to rush for more than 1,000 yards as a rookie. The 1,105 he gained exceeded the output of each of the other three: Beattie Feathers (1,004 in 1934), Cookie Gilchrist (1,096 in 1962) and Paul Robinson (1,023 in 1968).

However, Brockington did not lead the league in rushing in 1971, finishing second to Denver's Floyd Little (1,133). It was not for lack of trying. A three-game stretch to start November vaulted the former Ohio State running back to the No. 1 spot, if only temporarily.

Brockington gained more than 100 yards on the ground in consecutive games against the Detroit Lions, Chicago Bears and Minnesota Vikings. Those three teams – and the Packers – composed the NFC Central Division, also known as the Black and Blue Division.

The three-game stretch gave Green Bay (2-4) an opportunity to make inroads against the Vikings (5-1), Lions (4-2) and Bears (4-2). That the Packers went 1-1-1 against their rivals is one reason they failed to contend for the playoffs during Dan Devine's first season as head coach.

On November 1, Brockington bolted to 111 yards on 16 carries in a driving rain at Milwaukee County Stadium. His 41-yard burst set up Green Bay's first touchdown in a 14-14 tie with the Lions.

Six days later, in a 17-14 win over Chicago, Brockington's workload nearly doubled. He carried 30 times for 142 yards and a score.

With the game tied late, he bucked the line five consecutive times. In doing so, he set up Lou Michaels's game-winning, 22-yard field goal with 59 seconds left.

Brockington completed his personal trifecta on November 14 when he helped himself to a career-high 149 yards rushing in Minneapolis. The Packers more than tripled the Vikings' offensive output (301 to 87), but second-half turnovers doomed them and they lost 3-0.

Though the Packers didn't move up in the standings, their roving rookie shined. Brockington amassed 402 rushing yards, authored a dozen runs of 10 or more yards, and gleaned 17 rushing first downs during the three-game divisional derby.

"Brockington is as fine a runner as I've seen," Vikings coach Bud Grant said. "He makes many of his own yards by bouncing off people and by accelerating with those quick bursts he has."

Brockington was particularly effective in the second quarter of the road games at Soldier Field in Chicago and the Metrodome in Minneapolis. Brockington rushed for 78 yards on 10 carries against the Bears and churned out 70 on eight trips against the Vikings.

After the victory over the Bears, Brockington offered this: "I just try to get as much out of every play as I can. My first objective is to get a first down – you have to control the ball. After you get the first down, you think about going all the way."

The 148 rushing yards is the most in back-to-back second quarters by any player in team history. In seven seasons with Green Bay (1971-77), Brockington gained more rushing yards in that period than in any other.

As a rookie, the big back staked out 375 second-quarter rushing yards. A year later, he cruised to 358. He piled up a career-best 454 in 1973.

Those productive second quarters helped Brockington surpass 1,000 yards rushing in each of his first three seasons. He became the first player in NFL history to do so.

In May 1974, Brockington was rewarded with a three-year, no-cut contract. He was eager to continue his run of 1,000-yard seasons.

"Personally, I'm going to again shoot for 1,500 yards," he said.

Brockington did get his 1,500, but it took him three seasons to do it. From 1974 through 1976, he amassed 1,723 yards, a far less impressive total than that of his record-setting start.

Many reasons have been advanced to explain Brockington's slide – coaching turnover, his no-cut contract, personnel changes, the pounding he took, the loss of his favorite play. Many factors likely played a role.

In the end, Brockington had become a shell of the player he had been. The man who rushed for 50 or more yards a team-record nine times in the second quarter mustered only 25 overall in the 1977 season opener, his last game as a Packer.

He was waived three days later to make room for fullback Jim Culbreath. At the time, Brockington's 5,024 yards rushing were second-most in team history.

Three Years Running

Packers rookies who went on to amass the most rushing yards in their first three seasons with the team.

Player, Years	Att.	Yards	Avg.	LG	TD
John Brockington, 1971-1973	755	3,276	4.34	53	15
Eddie Lacy, 2013-2015	717	3,075	4.29	60	23
Jim Taylor, 1958-1960	402	1,800	4.48	32	18
Terdell Middleton, 1977-1979	450	1,708	3.80	t76	13
Gerry Ellis, 1980-1982	384	1,633	4.25	29	10
Brent Fullwood, 1987-1989	389	1,578	4.06	38	17
Edgar Bennett, 1992-1994	398	1,387	3.48	t39	14
Jessie Clark, 1983-1985	305	1,336	4.38	80	9
Paul Hornung, 1957-1959	281	1,310	4.66	72	12
Howie Ferguson, 1953-1955	327	1,269	3.88	57	4
Donny Anderson, 1966-1968	292	1,267	4.34	42	13
Walt Schlinkman, 1946-1948	318	1,259	3.96	44	8

Second-Quarter Receiving

Career
Packers who caught more than 125 second-quarter passes.

No.	Player	Yards	Avg.	LG	TD
211	Donald Driver	2,895	13.72	t82	19
*170	Don Hutson	2,834	16.67	t78	40
166	Sterling Sharpe	2,208	13.30	t79	23
143	Jordy Nelson	1,982	13.86	t93	22
142	James Lofton	2,757	19.42	t80	11
142	Randall Cobb	1,552	10.93	47	10
136	Greg Jennings	1,913	14.07	t64	17
126	Ahman Green	1,042	8.27	48	9

*Hutson's career numbers (excluding TDs) are incomplete.

Season
Packers who caught more than 30 second-quarter passes in a season.

No.	Player, Year	Yards	Avg.	LG	TD
36	Robert Brooks, 1995	651	18.08	t99	7
34	Sterling Sharpe, 1993	373	10.97	t37	4
34	Randall Cobb, 2014	469	13.79	47	5
33	Davante Adams, 2018	340	10.30	30	3
32	Sterling Sharpe, 1992	412	12.88	t76	6
31	Edgar Bennett, 1994	252	8.13	40	2

Game
Packers who caught six or more second-quarter passes in a game.

No.	Player, Date	Yards	Avg.	LG	TD
8	Don Hutson, Oct. 8, 1944	118	14.75	25	1
7	Don Hutson, Oct. 18, 1942	104	14.86	23	0
7	Don Hutson, Nov. 22, 1942	59	8.43	15	2
7	Sterling Sharpe, Dec. 20, 1992	93	13.29	18	2
7	Dorsey Levens, Sept. 13, 1998	42	6.00	9	0
7	Donald Driver, Nov. 10, 2002	92	13.14	38	0
6	Don Hutson, Oct. 7, 1945	144	24.00	t59	4
6	Max McGee, Oct. 14, 1962	117	19.50	t55	2
6	James Lofton, Oct. 15, 1984	87	14.50	20	0

2nd Quarter Receiving

Don Hutson
1935 - 1945

Don Hutson (14) turns upfield with a pass reception during the second quarter of Green Bay's 27-14 loss at City Stadium to the Cleveland Rams in 1945. (Photo courtesy of the Green Bay Press-Gazette)

The prediction would have been stunningly accurate had one word been different. Instead, the prognostication faded as quickly as the identity of the man who uttered it.

In the spring of 1942, Don Hutson reportedly crossed paths with a long-haired gentleman in a café. The stranger insisted on divining the fortune of Green Bay's leading receiver by reading tea leaves.

The mysterious man claimed Hutson would have his greatest season in 1945. Had the long-forgotten soothsayer substituted the word quarter for season, his bold forecast would have stood the test of time.

Hutson did stand out in 1945, just as he had in 10 previous seasons. He led the league in receptions for an NFL-record eighth time with 47, and he finished second in scoring (97 points) and in receiving touchdowns (nine).

But to say that the 1945 campaign was his greatest is open to debate.

What cannot be argued is Hutson's huge haul in the Packers' first meeting with the Detroit Lions that October. His second quarter that afternoon was his most fruitful.

Green Bay annihilated Detroit 57-21 at State Fair Park in West Allis. A 41-point explosion in the 15 minutes leading to halftime ignited the point pourri.

Don Hutson gets tackled by Marshall Goldberg after catching a pass against the Chicago Cardinals at City Stadium on November 1, 1942. (Photo courtesy of the Green Bay Press-Gazette)

The Packers ran just eight offensive plays in that second quarter. The team chalked up five receiving touchdowns (Hutson had four) and counted one on an interception return by Ted Fritsch.

Four receiving touchdowns in 15 minutes of play? It was pure Hutson, as no other player in team annals has had more than two in any one quarter.

Hutson hit pay dirt on catches of 59, 46, 17 and 6 yards. He hauled in two other non-scoring passes for 5 and 11 yards.

That's six passes for 144 yards and four touchdowns, all airmailed from the arm of Roy (Tex) McKay. Hutson's receiving yardage remained the team record for one quarter until October 1956, when Bill Howton grabbed five for 168.

Throw in the five extra points Hutson kicked, and the incomparable end scored an NFL-record 29 points in one quarter against the Lions.

"I never saw such an exhibition of touchdown passes in my life," said Gus Dorais, the Lions' head coach. "That was the ballgame. Outside of that, we played 'em nip and tuck."

Detroit was no pushover. It had won six straight and went on to defeat Green Bay 14-3 at season's end to finish a game ahead of the Packers in the standings.

Throughout his 11-year career (1935-45), the second quarter was Hutson's wheelhouse. His receiving efforts in that period were far greater than elsewhere.

Because play-by-plays do not exist for all the games in which he participated, Hutson's quarter-by-quarter receiving totals cannot be determined exactly. The speedy end caught at least 170 passes for 2,834 yards in the second quarter. That's far better than the first quarter – his next best quarter – in which he hauled in a minimum of 108 catches for 1,897 yards.

A breakdown by quarter of his receiving TDs provides the best illustration of Hutson's second-quarter prowess. The numbers are accurate, complete and eye-opening. From first quarter to last, he caught 22, 40, 11 and 26 touchdown passes.

Why such a bonanza in that particular period?

Hutson played in 117 regular-season games, but only made 60 starts (see end note). That meant there were a number of games in which he played little or not at all in the early going.

Other times, Hutson's work ended early. In the blowout of the Lions, he didn't play in the second half except to kick extra points. In New York in 1943, he was done after snaring seven passes for 72 yards in the first half.

In each of his final four seasons (1942-45), Hutson caught more passes in the second quarter than in any other. His most productive seasons were 1942, where he snagged at least 28 passes for 508 yards, and 1945, where he grabbed 24 for 451.

During his Hall of Fame career, Hutson collected 100 or more yards receiving in a single quarter seven times. Six of those outings occurred in the second quarter.

Green Bay was unbeaten (7-0) when he did so.

How talented was Hutson? Then, as today, writers struggled to describe his athletic ability.

Here's what Henry McLemore wrote in 1940: "Hutson is the greatest pass receiver who ever lived. He is the only man who ever played who could have made the Venus de Milo a reputation as a pass thrower."

Hutson's final go-round in 1945 almost didn't happen. In late summer of that year, he declared that the College All-Star Game of Aug. 30 would be his last.

The lanky end did not play in any of Green Bay's exhibition games. But days before the opener against the Bears, the Alabama Antelope reconsidered, returning for a memorable swan song that included the greatest quarter of his career.

End note

Green Bay, as did other teams, sometimes tested a defense before putting in their best players. The question then becomes, how much more dominant could Hutson have been had he played every game from the get-go?

Second-Quarter Passing

Career
Packers who threw for 2,500 or more second-quarter yards in their career.

Name	Att	Com	Yds	TD	HI	Rate
Brett Favre	2,734	1,656	18,978	142	91	84.93
Aaron Rodgers	1,600	1,032	11,754	100	21	101.81
Bart Starr	926	521	6,822	45	38	78.77
Lynn Dickey	846	475	6,421	50	50	75.57
Don Majkowski	426	235	2,644	12	15	68.63
Tobin Rote*	434	188	2,594	26	35	49.45

* Rote's totals (excluding TD passes) are higher. There are five games for which complete information does not exist.

Season
Packers who threw for 1,250 or more second-quarter yards in a season.

Name, Season	Att	Com	Yds	TD	HI	Rate
Brett Favre, 1997	193	118	1,536	15	10	90.51
Brett Favre, 1995	174	108	1,444	14	2	110.42
Aaron Rodgers, 2014	170	109	1,371	15	0	118.53
Brett Favre, 2007	174	112	1,313	8	4	92.91
Aaron Rodgers, 2008	152	106	1,282	12	4	110.69
Brett Favre, 1994	177	110	1,280	12	5	94.83
Brett Favre, 2004	174	108	1,273	10	5	91.48
Aaron Rodgers, 2011	160	105	1,268	12	2	109.58

Game
Packers who threw for more than 175 second-quarter yards in a game.

Name, Date	Att	Com	Yds	TD	HI	Rate
Aaron Rodgers, Nov. 9, 2014	13	9	242	4	0	151.46
Aaron Rodgers, Nov. 13, 2016	20	16	209	2	1	122.71
Aaron Rodgers, Sept. 15, 2013	17	15	197	2	0	154.17
Brett Favre, Nov. 10, 2002	21	13	190	1	0	107.24
Bart Starr, Oct. 23, 1966	6	5	181	1	0	158.33
Aaron Rodgers, Nov. 21, 2010	20	13	181	2	0	127.29
Matt Flynn, Jan. 1, 2012	12	9	180	2	1	121.53
Aaron Rodgers, Nov. 22, 2009	21	15	178	2	0	128.67
Scott Tolzien, Nov. 10, 2013	21	14	176	0	1	72.72

2nd Quarter Passing

Brett Favre
1992 - 2007

Brett Favre drops back to pass as he did for 16 seasons as a Green Bay Packer. (Chip Manthey photo)

Brett Favre had perfect attendance during a 16-year career spent schooling defenses.

The iron man of quarterbacks started 253 straight regular-season games for the Packers from 1992 through 2007. It's a franchise record for a player regardless of position.

Favre showed up like clockwork not because he was indestructible. The Hall of Famer endured his share of injuries. Ailing or not, Favre always punched in for work. He wouldn't have had it any other way.

"The thing that I'm most impressed about in my career is the fact that I've played in all those games. Whether it be consecutive or not, the fact that I played in that many games is amazing," Favre said at his retirement press conference in March 2008.

Of course, Favre didn't stay retired at that time. He returned to play one season with the New York Jets and another two with the Minnesota Vikings before calling it quits for good.

Favre holds most of the Packers' career passing records. He is No. 1 in attempts (8,754), completions (5,377), yards (61,655) and touchdown passes (442).

During his stay in Green Bay, he threw for more yards than every team except the Rams, Colts and Vikings. He attempted more passes than all but the Patriots, Cardinals and Rams.

Most striking: no team could match his TD output from 1992 through 2007. The Colts (403) came closest, but were still 39 short of Favre's prodigious total.

In answering in the affirmative at every roll call, Favre became Green Bay's second-quarter career leader as well. His numbers there – 2,734 attempts, 1,656 completions, 18,978 yards, 142 touchdowns – are all team records.

Favre was busiest in the second quarter during the 1997 season. He completed 118 of 193 passes for 1,536 yards with 15 touchdowns and 10 interceptions.

Favre threw for more than 1,000 second-quarter yards in 14 different seasons. He came up short only in 1993 and 2000.

The Gunslinger of Green Bay was in peak form as the Packers opened the 1996 campaign. The numbers he produced in Tampa Bay and against the Philadelphia

Brett Favre and head coach Mike Holmgren enjoy a victory at Lambeau Field. (Photo courtesy of the Green Bay Press-Gazette)

Eagles and San Diego Chargers at home rank among the best of any three-game stretch of his career.

No one was quite sure what to expect from Favre as the opener approached. It had been a trying offseason for the quarterback in more ways than one. Favre announced in May he had become addicted to painkillers. He spent 46 days in a Kansas drug rehabilitation clinic. In July, Favre's best friend, Mark Haverty, died when the van in which he was a passenger was hit by a train. The driver of the van was Favre's brother, Scott.

"For those doubters, if you're dead set on Brett Favre collapsing, then just bet against me, because you'll lose your money in the end," the competitive quarterback declared in late August. "That's the way I feel. That's how confident I am."

Green Bay rallied around its leader. It was time to make a Super Bowl run.

The Packers knocked off Tampa Bay 34-3 on the road. The team then crushed Philadelphia 39-13 and San Diego 42-10 at Lambeau Field.

Only once before, in 1961, had the team won three straight games by at least 25 points each and Favre became the first Packers quarterback to throw 10 TD passes in the first three games of a season. His passer rating ballooned to a league-best 122.0.

The Green and Gold rolled up more than 150 yards in three consecutive second quarters for the first time. The team amassed nearly three times the yardage (533) of its competitors (179) in the period.

Favre had his foot squarely on the gas pedal. He threw for 396 yards and five touchdowns in the second quarter to earn a passer rating of 126.7.

The fast start propelled Green Bay to a 13-3 record. In January 1997, the Packers defeated the New England Patriots 35-21 to win their first Super Bowl in nearly 30 years.

Favre had proven he could win it all. He had backed up his preseason bravado.

"I kind of put my foot in my mouth," Favre said when reminded of his preseason proclamation as the team celebrated its win over New England. "There was a little pressure on us after I said that. But I felt we were a good football team. And I thought I would come back and play as well as I ever did."

The second quarter was not Favre's greatest from a ratings standpoint. From first to last, Favre's ratings by quarter were 89.3, 84.9, 90.6 and 78.5.

But the 15-minute stretch before halftime was his most prolific. Favre threw for more yards in that period than any other in 13 of his 16 seasons in Green Bay.

Favre's last regular-season pass as a Packer came against the Detroit Lions on December 30, 2007, at Lambeau Field. Fittingly, his final offering was a 4-yard touchdown toss to tight end Bubba Franks early in the second quarter to put Green Bay up 21-10.

Craig Nall replaced Favre in the second half. Head coach Mike McCarthy rested Favre in the second half with his team having locked up the No. 2 seed in the NFC playoffs.

It was a rare break for a quarterback who refused to let anything prevent him from the highly entertaining field studies he conducted week after week without fail.

Second-Quarter Scoring

Career
Packers who scored more than 150 points in the second quarter.

Points	Name	TDs	PAT	FG
456	Mason Crosby	0	162-164	98-122
363	Ryan Longwell	0	117-117	82-104
319	Don Hutson	42	55-59	4-7
282	Chris Jacke	0	87-89	65-87
211	Paul Hornung	13	52-54	27-42
181	Chester Marcol	0	49-51	44-74
162	Fred Cone	6	60-64	22-33
162	Jim Taylor	27	0-0	0-0

Season
Packers who scored 50 or more points in the second quarter of one season.

Points	Name, Season	TDs	PAT	FG
65	Don Hutson, 1945	8	14-16	1-2
63	Don Hutson, 1942	8	12-12	1-1
58	Paul Hornung, 1961	7	10-10	6-7
53	Paul Hornung, 1964	4	14-16	5-9
51	Ryan Longwell, 2002	0	15-15	12-13
51	Mason Crosby, 2013	0	9-9	14-16
50	Mason Crosby, 2009	0	17-17	11-13

Game
Packers who scored more than 12 points in the second quarter of a game.

Points	Name, Date	TDs	PAT	FG
29	Don Hutson, Oct. 7, 1945	4	5-5	0-0
15	Paul Hornung, Nov. 12, 1961	2	3-3	0-0
14	Don Hutson, Oct. 11, 1942	2	2-2	0-0
14	Don Hutson, Nov. 1, 1942	2	2-2	0-0
14	Don Hutson, Nov. 22, 1942	2	2-2	0-0
14	Don Hutson, Oct. 28, 1945	2	2-3	0-0
13	Bob Monnett, Sept. 16, 1934	2	1-2	0-0
13	Clarke Hinkle, Nov. 13, 1938	2	1-1	0-0

2nd Quarter Scoring

Ryan Longwell
1997 - 2005

Ryan Longwell (8) celebrates after making a 54-yard field goal in the second quarter against the Tennessee Titans on December 16, 2001. (Photo courtesy of the Green Bay Press-Gazette)

Ryan Longwell wasn't supposed to be kicking field goals for the Packers in 1997. But the waiver-wire acquisition did his job so well and for so long that he all but rendered forgotten the name of the player who was.

Longwell played nine seasons (1997-2005) in Green Bay. He scored more than 100 points in each of his first eight seasons and became the first Packer to score more than 1,000 career points.

Not bad for a player who was supposed to be nothing more than a camp leg.

Brett Conway, not Longwell, was the Packers' choice to replace veteran Chris Jacke, who departed after the 1996 season. The team was so enamored with Conway that it selected him 90th overall in the 1997 draft. Conway was the only kicker among the 240 picks made that year.

Conway spent two training camps (1997 and 1998) with the Packers. He never played a regular-season game with the team.

Longwell entered the picture after the Packers put in a claim for him on July 10, 1997. The 49ers opted to keep veteran Gary Anderson over the rookie from California.

Getting cut didn't appear to affect Longwell's confidence. He declared himself ready to make the most of his newfound opportunity with the Packers.

"I thought we (he and Conway) were the two (kickers) who were heads and shoulders above everyone else at the combine," Longwell said. "When the Packers picked me up, they told me they'd help me catch on with someone if they could."

That Conway might not be as good as advertised became apparent in Green Bay's second preseason game, a 7-3 win over New England. Conway pushed three field goal attempts – from 32, 44, and 40 yards – wide to the right.

Conway was dealt another setback when he injured his right quadriceps during warmups before the team's third preseason game at Oakland. Longwell filled in and went 3-for-3 hitting from 21, 44 and 34 yards out.

Packers head coach Mike Holmgren remained in Conway's corner.

"Brett's going to be our kicker," he declared the day after Green Bay defeated the Raiders 37-24.

With Conway unable to compete, the Packers made the unusual move of keeping two kickers on their opening-day roster. Two days later, Conway was placed on injured reserve.

For better or worse, Longwell was the Packers' placekicker.

"It's a little better for me now to know that they have the confidence to go with me through the year," Longwell said. "But I won't change my approach."

Longwell scored 120 points in 1997. He connected on 24 of 30 field goals (80 percent).

Only Chester Marcol, with 128 points in 1972, had scored more points for the team as a rookie.

Even so, Longwell was not handed the kicking job in 1998. He and Conway again competed in camp. That is until August 21, 1998, when Green Bay traded Conway to the New York Jets. Longwell had prevailed.

From 1997 through 2005, Longwell scored 1,054 points for the Green and Gold. Only Jason Elam of the Broncos posted more during those nine years.

Longwell connected on 226 of 277 field goal attempts. His success rate of 81.6 remains the team record.

The second quarter was Longwell's most eventful. From first quarter to fourth, he tallied 190, 363, 210 and 282 points. He scored nine points in overtime on three field goals.

Longwell attempted 104 field goals in the second quarter, far more than he did in the first (45), third (57) or fourth (68) quarters. He also made more three-point kicks (82) than he did in the first (38), third (43) or fourth (60) periods.

To be fair, his second-quarter success rate (.788) was his third poorest behind that of the fourth (.882) and first (.844).

> *"When the Packers picked me up, they told me they'd help me catch on with someone if they could."*
>
> - Ryan Longwell

But never was his leg more accurate from long distance than in the second period. He nailed 9-of-13 kicks (69.2 percent) from 50 yards and beyond.

In the other three quarters combined, Longwell was merely 4-of-9 (44.4 percent).

On December 16, 2001, Longwell drilled a 54-yard field goal on the final play of the second quarter against the Tennessee Titans. His effort tied Chris Jacke's then-team record set in 1994.

"I just went out and swung away," Longwell said of his personal best. "I had great protection and a great hold (from backup quarterback Doug Pederson), and the Lord kept it in the air long enough for it to get there."

Green Bay came up short, 26-20 that evening. The team, however, never lost another game (nine straight) in which Longwell closed out the first half with a field goal.

During his Packers career, Longwell connected on 15-of-18 (.833) time-expiring, second-quarter, field goal attempts. He hit his last 10 in a row, starting with that 54-yarder at Tennessee.

Longwell led the team in second-quarter scoring outright in all nine of his seasons in Green Bay. He was most productive in 2002, when he scored 51 points by converting 12-of-13 field goal attempts.

He also never missed an extra point in the second quarter, hitting 117 straight.

Longwell signed with Minnesota as a free agent on March 11, 2006. He spent six seasons with the Vikings before calling it a career.

Halftime

Packers co-founder George Whitney Calhoun (shorter man in left-center of photo) is honored at halftime of the Packers-49ers game at old City Stadium on November 18, 1956. Calhoun was recognized for his many years of service to the team and was given a lifetime NFL pass, a Packers blanket, a gold watch, and other gifts. (Photo courtesy of the Green Bay Press-Gazette)

Half-Life Rushing

Ahman Green's first carry of 2001 was a poor indicator of the record-breaking first quarter to come.

Quicker than Green could juke a defender, the routine turned anything but as the Packers swamped the Detroit Lions in a flood of yards and points that outpaced the rain falling on Lambeau Field.

Green Bay appeared in mid-season form that September day as it unleashed 220 yards of total offense the first three times it had the ball. In less than 11 minutes, the Packers had pounced 21-0.

Green played a major role in amassing that early bounty. After gaining a mere three yards on his first try, he ripped off 31 yards and a touchdown on his second. He plowed ahead for five more yards on his third attempt, and his fourth venture covered 83 yards and resulted in the Packers' third score.

"Green Bay made the plays," Lions coach Marty Mornhinweg said after his team lost 28-6. "Green Bay made, geez, in the first half, made three or four big, big plays. We didn't, and all of a sudden it is 21-0."

Never had Detroit fallen behind by 21 points so quickly to start a season. Never had Green Bay scored three touchdowns with such speed to open a season.

Green rushed for 122 yards in the first quarter to help precipitate the deluge. By halftime, his total had swelled to 133. It was the second of six first halves in his Packers career in which he exceeded 100 yards rushing, a team record.

Ahman Green rushed for 100 or more yards in a half a record nine times for the Packers. (Photo courtesy of the Green Bay Press-Gazette)

The NFL record book first included an entry for 100-yard rushing days in its 1965 edition. Cleveland's Jim Brown headed the list, followed by the Packers' Jim Taylor.

To this day, gaining 100 or more yards rushing remains an accomplishment worth celebrating, but grabbing 100 in a half is a much greater challenge.

Surpassing 100 yards rushing in a game has been done more than 200 times in Packers history. More than 50 players have climbed that mountain at least once. On average, such performances occur twice or so a season.

Far more scarce are half-life 100s. Eighteen players have gained 100 or more yards rushing in one half for the Packers. In total, 36 cases have occurred, or about one every third year.

Andy Uram was Green Bay's first. He needed just two carries to get there.

On October 8, 1939, Green Bay hosted the Chicago Cardinals at State Fair Park in West Allis. The team's running game got a shot in the arm when Uram entered the game for the first time in the third quarter.

The sophomore running back picked up 11 yards on his first try. He weaved 97 yards for a touchdown on his second.

George Stickler of the *Chicago Tribune* wrote: "Frank Patrick, who played the outstanding game of his two year professional career, hit the former Gopher (Uram) squarely and had him firmly in his grasp. Other backs, believing such a perfect tackle final, eased up. Patrick relaxed his shoulder and Uram leaped up to continue on down the field."

In two tries, Uram had 108 yards rushing. He didn't get another carry in the Packers' 27-20 win over the Cardinals.

Breezy Reid was the next to produce 100 rushing yards in a half. He did so in the final two quarters as Green Bay edged the Baltimore Colts 35-24 on Halloween 1953.

Half-Life Runners

Packers who rushed for 100 or more yards in a half more than once.

Name	1st Half	2nd Half	Total
Ahman Green	6	3	9
Jim Taylor	2	5	7
Tom Moore	0	2	2
Dorsey Levens	0	2	2
Samkon Gado	2	0	2
Ryan Grant	1	1	2

In 1963, Jim Taylor became the first to chew up 100 in the opening 30 minutes. He staked out 115 yards in a 28-10 win over the San Francisco 49ers in Milwaukee.

Green's 133 yards against the Lions in the first two quarters of the 2001 opener are the most gained by any Packer in a first half. In 2003, Green set the record for a second half when he picked up 166 in the final two quarters in a 28-3 victory over the Denver Broncos.

The Packers' record when a back hits or exceeds 100 yards in the first half is 12-3. When such a feat occurs in the second half, the team is 18-3.

Half-Life Receiving

Bill Howton (right) shakes hands with Packers scout Jack Vainisi on May 5, 1952. Howton flew to Green Bay to sign his rookie contract that day. (Photo courtesy of the Green Bay Press-Gazette)

The Los Angeles Rams brought out the best in Bill Howton.

The offensive end caught more passes for more yards against the Rams than any other team during his seven seasons (1952-58) in Green Bay. His average per reception was an impressive 23.3 yards.

Howton went over 100 yards receiving four times in his first six games against the Rams. His best showing during that time was a six-catch, 200-yard performance at the Los Angeles Coliseum as a rookie in 1952.

He outdid himself in 1956. In a masterful display at Milwaukee County Stadium, Howton blew away what had been his personal best and required just one half of football to do so.

On October 21, 1956, Howton became the only Packer to earn more than 200 yards receiving in a half. The 204 yards he registered on six catches in the first two quarters were more than any NFL receiver gained in an entire game that season.

Howton figured prominently as Green Bay built a 21-10 lead. Four of his catches covered more than 35 yards, and two resulted in touchdowns.

In order, Howton snagged passes of 36, 36, 14, 11, 63 and 44 yards. Five came off the arm of Tobin Rote. The longest – the 63-yarder – was delivered by rookie first-round draft pick Jack Losch and completed the Packers' first-half scoring.

"He (Rote) and Bill Howton were spectacular," Packers coach Lisle Blackbourn raved. "The line gave Tobin good protection so he could get off those long ones."

Early in the fourth quarter, Howton caught one more pass – a 53-yarder – that Rote launched from his own end zone. That heave set the stage for yet another touchdown in Green Bay's 42-17 win.

Throughout the years, scores of Packers players have collected 100 or more yards receiving in a game. It's a rich tradition that dates at least to 1923, when Charlie Mathys caught eight for 123 yards against the Racine Legion.

Arriving at that total in one half is less common. Thirty-three players have achieved the milestone a total of 115 times.

Myrt Basing was first. His entire take against the Rochester Jeffersons in 1925 – three catches for 111 yards – came in the second half.

James Lofton did it most often. He went over 100 in one half a dozen times.

The half in which these yards are collected appears to make a difference. The Packers are 55-17-1 (.760) when a player hits the benchmark in the first half. The team is 21-20-1 (.512) when the feat is accomplished in the second half.

No one was better at getting out early than the immortal Don Hutson. The Alabama Antelope went over 100 yards 10 times in the first half, with Green Bay going 9-0-1 in those games.

Half-Life Receivers

Packers who caught passes for 100 or more yards in a half more than five times.

Name	1st Half	2nd Half	Total
James Lofton	5	7	12
Don Hutson	10	0	10
Sterling Sharpe	4	6	10
Bill Howton	6	3	9
Boyd Dowler	5	2	7
Antonio Freeman	4	3	7
Carroll Dale	5	1	6
Robert Brooks	6	0	6
Greg Jennings	5	1	6

The Third Quarter

Tobin Rote scrambles against the Detroit Lions in Green Bay on September 30, 1956. Rote threw for more than 3,000 yards in the third quarter during his seven seasons with the Packers. (Photo courtesy of the Green Bay Press-Gazette)

November 23, 1997

Dorsey Levens rushed for 190 yards against the Dallas Cowboys at Lambeau Field in 1997. Green Bay dominated Dallas in the third quarter and won going away, 45-17. (Photo courtesy of the Green Bay Press-Gazette)

Green Bay's November 23, 1997, meeting with Dallas was a circle-the-date type of affair. So big was the game that it would have been understandable had the Packers circled their wagons in order to prepare for it.

In the end, a more reasonable approach prevailed, and it worked. The Green and Gold ran circles around the Cowboys.

Dorsey Levens ran wild, setting a rushing record as the Packers thrashed Dallas 45-17. Levens's monster day and a remarkable third quarter paved the road to victory.

In order to understand the importance of this clash – at least from the Packers' point of view – one needs to take a look at earlier dust-ups between the two. The Cowboys had won eight straight against the Packers, including seven in a row in the heart of Texas.

The losses stung. Some more so than others.

On Thanksgiving Day 1994, Dallas rallied 42-31 behind third-string quarterback Jason Garrett. On November 18, 1996, the Cowboys won 21-6 as Chris Boniol toed an NFL-record-tying seven field goals, the last an unnecessary launch with just 20 seconds left.

Unable to win in Texas, the Packers longed for the day Dallas had to visit Lambeau Field. In 1997, the schedule makers obliged. Dallas was headed to Titletown for the first time since 1989.

While Green Bay focused on redemption, the Cowboys (6-6) just needed a win.

"What happened in the past has nothing to do with this game," Dallas head coach Barry Switzer said. "This is a big game for a lot of people. The people in Green Bay have had this one marked on their calendars for a long time."

Switzer claimed time of possession was one reason why Dallas had owned the Packers. The Cowboys had held the ball longer than Green Bay in each of their eight wins.

"That's our offensive philosophy, and that's why our playbook is built on ball control," he said. "But accomplishing that is hard against a good football team."

The Packers (8-3) were good. They were defending NFL champions, 10 months removed from having won their first Super Bowl in 29 years.

Now, they were looking to repeat. Dallas stood in the way.

"I don't want to say it's payback time," Levens said, "but it's about time we prove to ourselves that we can beat those guys."

As Levens went, so did the Green Bay ground game. The Packers' halfback ranked seventh in the league through 11 games with 939 rushing yards.

Levens outdid himself against the Cowboys. He commandeered 190 rushing yards on 33 carries to break Jim Taylor's franchise record of 186 yards.

Much of what he accomplished took place in the second half. Levens carried 11 times for 54 yards in the third quarter and ripped off 91 on 13 totes in the final 15 minutes.

Green Bay's groundswell allowed it to dominate Dallas in the third quarter. Brett Favre and the offense controlled the ball for 13 minutes, 8 seconds.

The Packers ran 25 plays. They recorded 11 first downs. They scored touchdowns on advances of 69 and 73 yards.

And Dallas? The overmatched Cowboys gained eight meaningless yards and had to punt as their three-and-out drive became a three-and-out quarter.

That's astonishing. Three-and-out quarters don't happen every week. The

Packers have held opponents to just three plays in one quarter eight times since 1953.

"This game was a tribute to an offensive line and a really tough running back," said Packers defensive coordinator Fritz Shurmur.

Linebacker Seth Joyner added: "The second half was something for the rest of the league to look at. If we keep rolling like that, the rest is history."

Green Bay, which held the ball for 37:19 against the Cowboys, did make it back to the Super Bowl. Unfortunately, the Denver Broncos ended the Packers' bid for two in a row with a 31-24 win.

The Third Quarter

It arrives after a brief intermission in which players, coaches and fans alike can collect their thoughts, recharge, and prepare for the final push.

The third quarter is the first quarter of the second half. It offers a fresh start. Fewer surprises remain as both teams have revealed at least some of their intentions in the first half.

That said, game plans might get tweaked. Adjustments may be implemented. How a team operates in the first 15 minutes following halftime can go a long way toward winning or losing.

Green Bay's dominance over the Cowboys remains one of its finest third quarters. There have been others.

> **October 26, 1958**—Babe Parilli becomes the first Packer to throw three touchdown passes in the third quarter. All three – to Al Carmichael, Gary Knafelc and Max McGee – are needed as Green Bay nearly squanders a 24-point lead before hanging on to beat the Philadelphia Eagles, 38-35, to register its only win of the season.
>
> **October 17, 1965**—Bart Starr rallies Green Bay from a 21-3 halftime deficit by pitching third-quarter scoring passes to Bob Long, Tom Moore and Carroll Dale. Starr provides the exclamation point with a 4-yard, fourth-quarter TD run to down the Detroit Lions 31-21 at Tiger Stadium.
>
> **December 10, 1972**—The Packers clinch the NFC Central Division title with a 23-7 victory over the Minnesota Vikings in frigid Minneapolis. Chester Marcol (field goal), Scott Hunter (rushing TD) and MacArthur Lane (rushing TD) deliver points on each of Green Bay's three third-quarter drives. Fred Carr (fumble recovery) and Willie Buchanon (two interceptions) ensure Minnesota is held scoreless in the period.

Third-Quarter Rushing

Career
Packers who rushed for more than 1,000 yards in the third quarter.

Yards	Player	Att.	Avg.	LG	TD
2,260	Jim Taylor	448	5.04	65	23
2,194	Ahman Green	432	5.08	t90	12
*1,141	Tony Canadeo	232	4.92	t50	6
1,108	Paul Hornung	244	4.54	63	10
1,042	Gerry Ellis	215	4.85	t39	9
1,033	Dorsey Levens	267	3.87	36	6

*Estimate based on the information available.

Season
Packers who rushed for more than 350 third-quarter yards in a season.

Yards	Player, Year	Att.	Avg.	LG	TD
469	Jim Taylor, 1962	67	7.00	51	7
464	Ahman Green, 2001	86	5.40	t63	4
408	Ahman Green, 2003	75	5.44	47	2
368	Ahman Green, 2004	64	5.75	t90	2
363	Dorsey Levens, 1999	76	4.78	36	2
351	Terdell Middleton, 1978	75	4,68	t76	5

Game
Packers who rushed for more than 80 yards in the third quarter of a game.

Yards	Player, Date	Att.	Avg.	LG	TD
109	Howie Ferguson, Oct. 2, 1955	3	36.33	57	0
108	Andy Uram, Oct. 8, 1939	2	54.00	t97	1
107	Ahman Green, Oct. 24, 2004	4	26.75	t90	1
90	Ed Cody, Oct. 26, 1947	6	15.00	51	1
85	Billy Grimes, Oct. 8, 1950	2	42.50	t61	1
84	Tom Moore, Nov. 20, 1960	4	21.00	t59	1
84	Eddie Lacy, Nov. 4, 2013	7	12.00	56	1
83	Jessie Clark, Sept. 29, 1985	3	27.67	80	1
81	Terdell Middleton, Oct. 1, 1978	3	27.00	t76	1

3rd Quarter Rushing

Tony Canadeo
1941 - 1944, 1946 - 1952

Tony Canadeo picks up a first down in the third quarter of Green Bay's 35-14 win over the Chicago Cardinals in 1943. Ronnie Cahill makes the tackle for the Cardinals. (Photo courtesy of the Green Bay Press-Gazette)

Tony Canadeo's rushing totals may have been even greater had Dorothy Mann been in attendance for all of his games with the Packers.

Certainly the dependable halfback profited from her presence as he closed out his eighth season as a professional.

On December 11, 1949, Mann sat in the stands along with 12,575 others at Briggs Stadium in Detroit. There, the Lions (3-8) and Packers (2-9) skirmished to determine whether one or both would finish last in the Western Division standings.

Mann was especially keen on the play of No. 87 for the Lions. That jersey number belonged to her husband, end Bob Mann.

Bob Mann was credited with eight catches for 182 yards and two touchdowns in Detroit's 21-7 win. But Dorothy was sure Bob had caught nine, and she let the powers that be know.

Lions management re-examined the play-by-play. Indeed, Bob and quarterback Frank Tripucka had collaborated nine, not eight, times. Dorothy, armed with nothing more than pencil and paper, had been correct.

The review also revealed that Canadeo had been shortchanged by 12 yards. His rushing output for the season jumped to 1,052.

Canadeo was one of the few bright spots for the Packers in 1949. Curly Lambeau's last hurrah as head coach was hardly worth celebrating as the team won but two games.

One area of strength was the team's running game. Led by Canadeo, the Packers ran for 2,061 yards, the fourth-highest total among the league's 10 teams.

That pounding the ball would become Green Bay's principal mode of transportation became evident in the season opener. Passers Jug Girard, Stan Heath and Jack Jacobs failed to complete even one pass in 13 tries as the Packers succumbed 17-0 to the Bears.

Everything the Green and Gold earned that day (187 yards) came out of the backfield. Canadeo led all runners with 92 yards on 11 tries.

Chicago head coach George Halas took notice.

"And you talk about that 'old' Canadeo," he marveled, "He took that ball and, BOOM, he was out in the clear. He's a terrific player."

The boom Halas was likely referring to was Canadeo's 37-yard dash. It brought the ball to the Chicago 25-yard line early in the second quarter. The promising drive ended after Girard tossed the first of three Packers interceptions.

Canadeo hit or exceeded 100 yards rushing an NFL-best five times in 1949. He got there against the New York Bulldogs (100), Los Angeles Rams (122), Detroit Lions (117), Pittsburgh Steelers (116) and Chicago Cardinals (122).

Green Bay relied heavily on Canadeo in 1949. He carried at least 15 times on eight occasions. Canadeo was utilized to that extent just seven times in his other 10 seasons combined.

Though he held the upper hand for much of the season, Canadeo did not lead the league in rushing in 1949. That honor went to the Eagles' Steve Van Buren, who finished with 1,146 yards. The two runners were so far ahead of the field that no player finished within 350 yards of them.

Canadeo's record-setting season was unique, and not just because he was the first Packer to surpass 1,000 yards rushing in a season. His age, his role, his team, and the scoreboard made his accomplishment all the more remarkable.

Canadeo is the only Packer to have surpassed 1,000 yards in his thirties. The eight others who did – Jim Taylor, John Brockington, Terdell Middleton, Edgar Bennett, Dorsey Levens, Ahman Green, Ryan Grant and Eddie Lacy – all were in their twenties.

Of that group, Canadeo is the only one who also had to play defense. Though not a regular on that unit, Canadeo turned defender on at least three occasions: against the Lions on October 30, the Bears on November 6, and the Giants on November 13.

Canadeo is the only 1,000-yarder for Green Bay to have played on such a win-starved team. The others all played for teams that won at least four games.

And finally, winning so infrequently meant that Canadeo did most of his running with the scoreboard working against him. Only 18 of his 208 rushing attempts – less than 10 percent – occurred with Green Bay out front. Astonishingly, the team ran its last 419 offensive plays of the year (sacks included) without holding a lead.

Though the team never seemed to get ahead, Canadeo flourished.

During his 11-year career (1941-44, 1946-52), Canadeo rushed for 4,197 yards. He passed Clarke Hinkle (3,860) for the No. 1 spot in franchise history on the final weekend of the 1950 season.

Canadeo's most productive quarter was the third. It is the only period in which it can be said with certainty that he accumulated more than 1,000 rushing yards.

Much of that was gained in 1949. He piled up more than 300 yards and averaged better than five yards a pop.

The bulk of that was accumulated during an eight-game stretch that began in New York's Polo Grounds in early October. Canadeo collected more than 40 third-quarter rushing yards as Green Bay blanked the Bulldogs 19-0. He then earned more than 20 yards in that period in each of the next seven games.

Canadeo's most productive third quarter ever likely occurred on October 3, 1948, against the Lions. He grabbed 59 yards – half of his 118-yard total for the day – as the Packers downed the Lions 33-21.

Always a fan favorite, Canadeo was honored when the team celebrated Tony Canadeo Day on November 23, 1952. The halfback was presented with an automobile and other gifts. Canadeo scored two touchdowns in Green Bay's 42-14 romp over the Dallas Texans that day. His second came on a 10-yard run in the third quarter.

The Packers benefitted from Canadeo's presence for years, but his influence didn't stop at the locker room door.

"I guess the best thing that happened to me was Tony Canadeo getting off to such a fine start and taking such a big lead on me in the ground gaining race," Van Buren said as the 1949 season was wrapping up. "I just began to run a wee bit harder."

Van Buren wasn't the last player impacted by Canadeo. Bob Mann got to know the running back better after he joined the Packers late in the 1950 season.

Third-Quarter Receiving

Career
Packers who caught 100 or more third-quarter passes.

No.	Player	Yards	Avg.	LG	TD
196	Donald Driver	2,787	14.22	t68	18
136	Sterling Sharpe	1,896	13.94	t58	9
134	Jordy Nelson	1,826	13.63	t80	14
130	James Lofton	2,266	17.43	t57	9
123	Antonio Freeman	1,782	14.49	63	13
105	Boyd Dowler	1,518	14.46	t50	7
104	Greg Jennings	1,812	17.42	t80	15

Season
Packers who caught more than 25 third-quarter passes in a season.

No.	Player, Year	Yards	Avg.	LG	TD
28	Sterling Sharpe, 1989	441	15.75	57	2
28	Donald Driver, 2006	461	16.46	t68	6
27	Sterling Sharpe, 1992	349	12.93	43	1
27	Donald Driver, 2007	272	10.07	26	0
27	Davante Adams, 2018	338	12.52	41	2
26	Antonio Freeman, 1998	356	13.69	44	3
26	Javon Walker, 2004	409	15.73	57	3
26	Donald Driver, 2005	385	14.81	59	1

Game
Sterling Sharpe is the only Packer to have caught more than five.

No.	Player, Date	Yards	Avg.	LG	TD
6	Sterling Sharpe, Oct. 4, 1992	74	12.33	24	1

3rd Quarter Receiving

Antonio Freeman
1995 - 2001, 2003

Antonio Freeman caught 123 third-quarter passes, all from quarterback Brett Favre. (Photo courtesy of the Green Bay Press-Gazette)

Antonio Freeman made headlines as a special teamer as a rookie. By the time his career came to an end, the veteran route runner had generated plenty of ink as a special pass catcher.

Freeman was Green Bay's go-to receiver during the second half of the 1990s. He led the team in receptions (137) during the club's back-to-back Super Bowl appearances following the 1996 and 1997 seasons.

~ 71 ~

In 1998, he produced a league-high 1,424 receiving yards. His 14 touchdowns through the air were second only to the 17 of rookie Randy Moss of Minnesota.

In eight years with Green Bay (1995-2001, 2003), Freeman caught 431 passes for 6,551 yards and 57 touchdowns. He was the fifth-leading receiving in team history at the time of his retirement.

Freeman was selected 90th overall by the Packers in the 1995 college draft. He was the ninth receiver to come off the board.

Once in Green Bay, the Virginia Tech product joined a crowded field at receiver. Eleven wideouts were on the roster for the preseason opener against New Orleans, in part because the team was searching to replace Sterling Sharpe, who had been forced to retire with a neck injury.

Fans first glimpsed Freeman's toughness during that game against the Saints. Twice he absorbed wicked hits, once on a punt return and once on a pass reception.

Freeman was Green Bay's leading receiver (10 catches) during the preseason in 1995. Even so, he was inactive or did not see action in four of the team's first eight regular-season games.

His ticket to playing time showed up in the punt return game. Freeman filled in for an injured Charles Jordan (separated shoulder) and played well enough to continue in that role despite Jordan's return to health.

"He (Freeman) might be one of the steals we had in the draft," head coach Mike Holmgren said in early November. "He's a talent. He's going to be active this week to return kicks for us. We have some good depth at wide receiver, otherwise he'd be active every week."

Freeman returned 37 punts for 292 yards in 1995. He broke Jeff Query's team record (30) for most returns as a rookie.

In 1996, Freeman became a starter at wide receiver and went on to start 90 of a possible 96 regular-season games from 1996 through 2001.

The third quarter was Freeman's most productive throughout his career. He caught more passes for more yards in that period (123 for 1,782 yards) than in the first (92 for 1,538), second (111 for 1,578) or fourth quarters (104 for 1,710).

Every reception Freeman made in the first three quarters originated from the arm of Brett Favre. Only in the final 15 minutes did Freeman accept throws from others, with three coming from Doug Pederson and two from Matt Hasselbeck.

Freeman is the only player in team history to have caught 100 or more receptions in a quarter with all of them coming from the same passer.

Freeman caught 20 or more third-quarter passes in each of four straight seasons: 1997 (23), 1998 (26), 1999 (20) and 2000 (20). Sixty-six of those 89 receptions brought first downs.

Twice Freeman caught five third-quarter passes in a game. He grabbed five for 57 yards and a touchdown in the Packers' 16-13 win in Chicago in 1998. He snagged five for 56 yards and a touchdown in a 27-18 loss to the Buffalo Bills in 2000.

In August 1999, Freeman was rewarded with a seven-year, $42-million contract. Ten million of the money was guaranteed.

"It was everything I hoped and dreamed of," he said. "I'm just happy to be a Green Bay Packer for a long, long time to come. I love it here. I always wanted to be here."

Freeman's numbers declined after his big payday. He went from 84 receptions in 1998 to 74 in 1999, 62 in 2000, and 52 in 2001.

Only once did Freeman gain 100 third-quarter receiving yards in a game. He caught three for 104 yards as Green Bay defeated Jacksonville 28-21 in 2001.

The Packers released Freeman on June 3, 2002, to save $4.3 million on the salary cap.

"He made a tremendous impact here in Green Bay and he will be missed," head coach Mike Sherman said.

Just over a year later, Freeman was back. Injuries to Donald Driver (neck) and Robert Ferguson (knee and ankle) in the 2003 season opener had the Packers contacting him while the game with the Vikings was still in progress.

"When I saw Driver hurt, I knew there was a slight chance my number could be called," Freeman said. "After knowing about Ferguson, I was almost sure that I would get the call."

Freeman caught 14 passes for 141 yards in 2003, his final year in Green Bay. He signed again with the team in June 2007 so he could retire as a Packer.

Third-Quarter Passing

Career
Packers who threw for 2,000 or more third-quarter yards in their career.

Name	Att	Com	Yds	TD	HI	Rate
Brett Favre	2,045	1,290	14,708	107	56	90.65
Aaron Rodgers	1,311	859	10,695	68	20	101.61
Bart Starr	718	409	5,626	30	26	81.04
Lynn Dickey	604	350	4,654	20	33	70.75
Tobin Rote*	406	191	3,002	26	19	73.94
Don Majkowski	411	222	2,676	14	12	73.41

Rote's totals (excluding TDs) are higher. There are five games for which complete information does not exist.

Season
Packers who threw for 1,000 or more third-quarter yards in a season.

Name, Season	Att	Com	Yds	TD	HI	Rate
Aaron Rodgers, 2011	123	82	1,382	12	0	136.97
Brett Favre, 1996	138	94	1,278	14	3	122.19
Aaron Rodgers, 2012	145	98	1,230	7	3	101.22
Aaron Rodgers, 2009	140	98	1,157	5	2	100.80
Don Majkowski, 1989	163	95	1,123	8	3	88.05
Aaron Rodgers, 2018	156	99	1,103	6	0	97.25
Brett Favre, 1997	132	84	1,011	9	3	100.28
Aaron Rodgers, 2016	148	99	1,010	3	2	87.39
Brett Favre, 1998	147	91	1,001	6	8	72.97

Game
Packers who threw for 150 or more third-quarter yards in a game.

Name, Date	Att	Com	Yds	TD	HI	Rate
Bart Starr, Oct. 17, 1965	8	7	225	3	0	158.33
Brett Favre, Dec. 3, 2001	15	11	179	2	0	152.50
Aaron Rodgers, Dec. 30, 2012	7	7	177	2	0	158.33
Aaron Rodgers, Nov. 24, 2011	11	9	173	1	0	149.05
Aaron Rodgers, Dec. 23, 2012	11	10	170	1	0	149.05
Aaron Rodgers, Nov. 1, 2009	14	12	169	2	0	156.55
Aaron Rodgers, Oct. 9, 2011	15	8	166	1	0	114.86

3rd Quarter Passing

Bart Starr
1956 - 1971

Bart Starr fires a pass in the direction of Boyd Dowler (far right) in a game against the Los Angeles Rams. (Photo courtesy of the Green Bay Press-Gazette)

Though he won more championships than any passer in Packers history, Bart Starr was unaccustomed to victory early in his career.

That he emerged as the quarterback who helmed the team's offense during the Glory Years of the 1960s is a testament to his dedication, patience and hard work.

Starr won five NFL championships during his 16-season career (1956-71). In the late 1950s, however, his name was just another entry on the team's roster.

The Packers drafted Starr in the 17th round in 1956. When camp opened in late July, he was expected to battle Lynn Beightol and Rod Hermes for the backup spot behind starter Tobin Rote.

Starr, Beightol and Hermes? Might as well have been the name of a law firm from what little was known about the three.

As a rookie, Starr made one start. He opened in a 17-16 loss to the San Francisco 49ers at old City Stadium, but gave way to Rote in the second quarter.

From 1957-60, Starr competed for playing time with fellow quarterbacks Babe Parilli, Joe Francis, Lamar McHan and others. During that time, Starr's shortcomings became known to anyone who could read a newspaper.

Starr's arm strength was questioned. After the 1957 opener, a game won by Green Bay 21-17, Chuck Johnson of *The Milwaukee Journal* wrote: "Starr started Sunday, but the stiff south wind affected his 'soft' passes and made them flutter and wobble. Parilli came in at the start of the second quarter and the Bears couldn't get him out the rest of the afternoon."

Starr's toughness remained in doubt. In November 1958, an unidentified teammate was quoted as saying: "It's just that he's got to get experience and meanness or cockiness or whatever you want to call it."

Starr could be inconsistent, but in this, at least, he was not alone.

"There is no consistency at quarterback," lamented Ray (Scooter) McLean in 1958 as his one-season disaster as head coach (1-10-1) neared the end. "I guess I have to find one that's hot for the day."

This pointing of fingers at the team's passers was widespread. As *Green Bay Press-Gazette* sports editor Art Daley noted: "The three most cussed and discussed gents in our town are the Packers' quarterbacks (Starr, Parilli and Francis)."

Columnist Jack Rickard was more blunt: "Green Bay will never be a winner with those two (Starr and Parilli)."

In his first three years, Starr was not credited with a victory by the press that covered the team. By today's measures, he was 3-15-1 as a starter over than span.

One voice that did not fault the quarterbacks completely belonged to Vince Lombardi. His opinion was one that counted, and he arrived at it after spending countless hours watching game film in the weeks that followed his hiring as Packers head coach in February 1959.

"I'm not convinced that the quarterbacks were entirely to blame for last year's poor offense," Lombardi said. "The offensive line didn't appear too strong."

Still, Lombardi wasn't bashful about sending a third-round draft choice in May to the Chicago Cardinals to get McHan. Clearly, Starr's quest to lead had not yet ended. McHan or Starr started all 24 regular-season games for Green Bay in 1959 and 1960. Starr's record (8-5) was comparable to that of McHan (7-4).

Of greater importance: Starr started the final seven games of 1960, a year that saw the Packers go 8-4 and finish first in the Western Conference. He was Lombardi's choice to quarterback the team in the championship game against the Philadelphia Eagles, a 17-13 loss.

In March 1961, McHan was traded to the Colts for an undisclosed draft choice. Nearly five years after entering the league, Starr was the Packers' quarterback for the foreseeable future.

Green Bay went on to capture NFL championships in 1961, 1962 and 1965-67. Starr's regular-season record was 69-18-4 over that span, and he was 9-0 in the playoffs. Rickard had been wrong. Starr was a winner.

On October 17, 1965, Starr engineered the greatest comeback of his career. The win came in a game in which the Packers (4-0) and Lions (3-1) battled with first place in the Western Conference on the line.

Starr had a less-than-stellar first half, hitting six of 10 passes for 48 yards. Defensive back Wayne Rasmussen intercepted one of his throws and returned it for a touchdown. Detroit led 21-3 at the break.

With his team down by 18, Lombardi delivered this message: "You're all Packers and you've got your pride. Stay in there and things will work out for you."

Message received. Green Bay scored touchdowns on each of its first three second-half possessions to go up 24-21 en route to a 31-21 victory. Starr threw eight times in the third quarter. He dissected the Lions with a cool, detached precision.

Starr's second, seventh and eighth passes reached the end zone. Bob Long (62 yards), Tom Moore (31) and Carroll Dale (77) served as couriers.

Long got behind defensive back Bobby Smith on the first TD. Dale delivered a downfield block on Rasmussen that gave Long the all-clear for the final 23 yards.

On the second, Moore had to twice shrug off would-be tacklers. Cornerback Dick LeBeau gave him one last jolt inside the five, but to no avail.

Dale had nothing but green grass to negotiate on his sprint to the end zone. His catch came on third-and-two when the Lions were expecting a run.

Starr's seven third-quarter completions stretched for 225 yards. A whopping 128 was earned after the catch on the three scores alone.

"Starr had himself a great, great game," Lombardi beamed. "He got undue pressure in the first half, but stayed right in there. He deserves a lot of credit."

The passing yards that afternoon were easily the most put up by Starr in any quarter of his career.

The third quarter was not Starr's greatest in terms of production. That was the second quarter, where he had the most attempts (926), completions (521), yards (6,822) and touchdowns (45) of any period.

But for Starr, the third quarter was his best when it came to avoiding interceptions. The 26 picks he tossed there were his fewest, as was the rate (3.6 percent) at which he threw them.

Starr didn't throw any third-quarter interceptions in both 1964 and 1966. He went 133 consecutive passes without one from 1963 to 1965.

Only twice in his career did Mr. Quarterback throw two interceptions in the same third quarter: November 2, 1958, in Baltimore and September 24, 1967, against the Bears. He was far more likely to toss multiple interceptions in other quarters: first (six times), second (four) and fourth (six).

Starr's 225 yards against the Lions was instrumental in making his 1965 third-quarter passing yardage (618) a career high for the period. He was more productive in just three other quarters over the course of a season: second quarter 1962 (789), second quarter 1961 (678) and second quarter 1965 (630).

The rally in Detroit helped propel Green Bay to a 10-3-1 record. The team then beat the Baltimore Colts 13-10 in overtime before knocking off the Cleveland Browns 23-12 to win its third NFL championship of the decade.

"I think I marked this team pretty well," said Lombardi. "I said this may not be the best team I've had, but it had the most character."

With Starr, character had never been a concern. From the start, it was evident this was one area in which he would never be found lacking.

Third-Quarter Scoring

Career

Packers who scored 100 or more points in the third quarter.

Points	Name	TDs	PAT	FG
321	Mason Crosby	0	114-116	69-82
210	Ryan Longwell	0	81-82	43-57
174	Chris Jacke	0	69-70	35-48
152	Paul Hornung	13	38-38	12-31
150	Jim Taylor	25	0-0	0-0
119	Don Hutson	14	32-36	1-1
112	Chester Marcol	0	34-35	26-38
*110	Donald Driver	18	0-0	0-0

*Driver had one 2-point conversion.

Season

Packers who scored 30 or more points in the third quarter of one season.

Points	Name, Season	TDs	PAT	FG
48	Mason Crosby, 2011	0	15-16	11-11
42	Jim Taylor, 1962	7	0-0	0-0
39	Paul Hornung, 1960	4	9-9	2-4
39	Ryan Longwell, 2000	0	6-6	11-12
36	Donald Driver, 2006	6	0-0	0-0
34	Mason Crosby, 2007	0	13-13	7-9
30	Terdell Middleton, 1978	5	0-0	0-0
30	Don Beebe, 1996	5	0-0	0-0
30	Ahman Green, 2001	5	0-0	0-0

Game

Packers who scored more than 12 points in the third quarter of a game.

Points	Name, Date	TDs	PAT	FG
14	Paul Hornung, Oct. 8, 1961	2	2-2	0-0
13	Don Hutson, Nov. 30, 1941	2	1-2	0-0

3rd Quarter Scoring

Mason Crosby
2007 - 2018

Mason Crosby booted a team-record 58-yard field goal in Minnesota against the Vikings in 2011. (Photo courtesy of the Green Bay Press-Gazette)

Pick a number. Any number.

Chances are whatever your selection, Mason Crosby was the fastest to score that many points in Packers history.

How about 100? Crosby got there first. He required just 12 games to hit that milestone, one more than runner-up Ryan Longwell.

How about 200? Crosby again arrived first, needing 24 games – or two fewer than second-place Longwell – to do so.

Five hundred? Crosby is first (63); Longwell is second (66).

One thousand? Crosby (124) is No. 1; Longwell (136) is No. 2.

Most, fastest, longest – those are words often associated with Crosby and kicking. Whatever the list, Crosby's name is likely at the top.

Crosby was selected 193rd overall by the Packers in the 2007 draft. He was the last of three kickers chosen that year.

In 12 seasons in Green Bay through 2018, Crosby scored a team-record 1,439 points. He became only the second player in league history (Jason Elam was the first) to score 100 or more points in each of his first 10 seasons in the league.

Shortly after Crosby was drafted, Packers special teams coach Mike Stock left a voicemail with incumbent kicker Dave Rayner. After listening to what Stock had to say, Rayner, who was on vacation in the Dominican Republic, turned to teammate Noah Herron and said: "This is not good."

Mason Crosby is the Packers' all-time scoring leader in every quarter. (Photo courtesy of the Green Bay Press-Gazette)

Rayner couldn't have been more correct. Competition between Rayner and Crosby was intense throughout training camp.

Mike Vandermause of the *Green Bay Press-Gazette* provided an update in mid-August. Crosby had made 85 percent of his field goal attempts (78-of-91), while Rayner had converted 81 percent (75-of-92).

The Packers released Rayner on September 1. Crosby was their kicker.

"Training camp and the competition with Dave helped me to push myself and get better," Crosby said. "I was confident and happy with how I was kicking and was hoping for the best, so this is kind of cool."

Crosby promptly went out and led the league in scoring. He set a franchise rookie scoring record with 141 points as he guided 31 of 39 field goal attempts through the uprights and was perfect on 48 extra point tries.

Those 141 points remain Crosby's single-season best. He also scored 141 points in 2013 when he nailed 33 of 37 field goal attempts and hit all 42 of his extra point kicks.

Crosby had scored 1,267 points after 10 years in the league. Only New England's Stephen Gostkowski had scored more (1,354) over that span.

In 2017, Crosby tallied a career-low 78 points. A year later, he bounced back with 124.

Crosby is the Packers' all-time scoring leader in every quarter. From first to fourth, he has scored 286, 456, 321 and 400 points.

Though not his most prolific quarter, the third is Crosby's most accurate as far as kicking field goals. His success rate of 84.15 percent in that period (69-of-82) is higher than his next best quarter, which is the second at 80.33 percent (98-of-122).

In 2011, Crosby was nearly flawless in the third quarter, holding true on all 11 of his field goal attempts and missing but one of 16 tries for extra point.

Included among those kicks were a couple of boomers. Both came in victory, and both were much needed.

On October 9, 2011, Crosby blasted a 56-yarder through the uprights in Atlanta's Georgia Dome. That effort tied the team record he had set a year earlier in the 2010 season opener, and the kick pulled Green Bay to within five points of the Falcons (14-9). The Packers won 25-14.

Two weeks later, Crosby drilled a 58-yarder indoors against the Vikings. His four field goals that afternoon helped topple Minnesota 33-27.

Crosby's only miss of 2011 popped up against the Raiders at Lambeau Field on December 11. With two minutes, 48 seconds remaining in the third quarter, defensive tackle Desmond Bryant blocked Crosby's try for extra point by leaping over long snapper Brett Goode. The breakdown did not impact the outcome, as Green Bay pummeled Oakland 46-16.

Crosby's 48 points in the third quarter in 2011 are a team record. He broke the mark of 42 set by Jim Taylor in 1962.

From late 2010 to early 2012, Crosby did not miss a third-quarter field goal attempt. His string of 16 consecutive successes is a personal best for one quarter.

The third quarter was Crosby's most accurate from long distance. He connected on 10-of-16 attempts (62.5 percent) from 50 or more yards in that period. The only other quarter in which he made more attempts than he missed was the second, in which he converted 13-of-21 (61.9 percent).

Crosby began the 2019 season having made his last eight field goal attempts in the third quarter. It marks the fifth time the kicker has had a run of at least eight straight third-quarter successes in his career.

The Fourth Quarter

Donald Driver celebrates with the Lambeau Field faithful after reaching the end zone on a 71-yard, fourth-quarter pass from Aaron Rodgers against the Detroit Lions in December 2008. (Photo courtesy of the Green Bay Press-Gazette)

October 17, 1983

Tight end Paul Coffman (82) and running back Gerry Ellis (31) shake hands during the Packers' thrilling 48-47 victory over the Washington Redskins on October 17, 1983. The game stood as the highest-scoring Monday Night Football game until 2018. (Photo courtesy of the Green Bay Press-Gazette)

On the evening of October 17, 1983, the eyes of the NFL turned to Green Bay, Wisconsin. Under the bright lights of Lambeau Field, the Packers and Washington Redskins erupted in an offensive explosion so powerful that it became an instant classic.

More than 55,000 fans watched the drama unfold from their seats in the historic stadium. Millions more tuned in to ABC's *Monday Night Football*.

Green Bay escaped that night with a 48-47 win. The final snap, which saw Washington kicker Mark Moseley send a 39-yard field goal attempt wide right, decided the outcome.

Ninety-five points and 1,025 yards of offense were generated during a free-for-all that lasted three hours, 16 minutes. The combatants gained nearly 10 yards every time they dropped back to pass.

Through three quarters, neither team could separate itself from the other. It would take the fourth quarter – all 900 seconds of it – to determine a winner.

"They played the Olympics early this year with Green Bay as the site," quipped Washington quarterback Joe Theismann. "I've never been in a game like this, and I hope I never am again."

The 1983 Packers gushed offense, unloading an impressive 6,172 yards and manufacturing a healthy 429 points, with the team surpassing 40 points four times.

Quarterback Lynn Dickey led the NFL with 4,458 passing yards. His favorite targets – James Lofton, John Jefferson and Paul Coffman – combined for 26 receiving TDs.

Defense – or lack thereof – also defined the 1983 Packers. Opponents racked up 6,472 yards. They piled up 439 points, a Packers' record for generosity.

In 1983, as in every year, the fourth quarter loomed large. Crunch time can spawn rallies, trigger collapses, or result in fantastic finishes. Fatigue rears its head. Urgency becomes heightened. Goats and heroes emerge.

And so it was against Washington. Five lead changes occurred in the final 15 minutes; 31 points were sowed; and not a punt or penalty spoiled the proceedings.

Five plays gained 25 yards or more. A total of 361 yards resulted.

The pace became so frenetic that the stats crew ceased listing tackles. No one was credited with having made a stop on Washington's final drive. Even the distance of Moseley's last-second kick was listed incorrectly as 37 yards instead of 39.

In pushing the ball right, Moseley was cast as the goat. That label had to sting for a kicker who, a year earlier, had been named Player of the Year with a success rate of 95.2 percent (20 of 21).

Determining a hero was not so easy. Dickey passed for 387 yards and three touchdowns. Linebacker Mike Douglass returned a fumble 22 yards to open the scoring. Jan Stenerud's 20-yard field goal ultimately provided the final points.

Given so many contributed, defensive end Ezra Johnson effused: "We got pride. We got desire. We got heart. We proved what kind of caliber of team we got."

That night at Lambeau Field was special. It prompted color commentator Don Meredith to quip: "The coaches had a meeting a while ago, and they decided the first team to 50 wins."

That entertaining finish was not Green Bay's only one. Here are three others:

> **October 23, 1921**—Art Schmael's plunge and Curly Lambeau's PAT propelled the Packers past Minneapolis 7-6 in their first league game ever.
>
> **September 27, 1959**—Jim Taylor's 5-yard TD run with 7:15 left and Dave Hanner's tackle of quarterback Ed Brown for a safety sent Green Bay to a 9-6 win over the Bears in Vince Lombardi's head-coaching debut.
>
> **September 20, 1992**—In his first action at quarterback in relief of an injured Don Majkowski, Brett Favre lofted a 35-yard strike to receiver Kitrick Taylor in the end zone to deliver a 24-23 win over the Cincinnati Bengals at Lambeau Field.

4th Quarter Rushing

Ahman Green
2000 - 2006, 2009

Ahman Green is the Packers' all-time rushing leader in the fourth quarter. (Photo courtesy of the Green Bay Press-Gazette)

No less an individual than Brett Favre watched in awe as the longest run in Packers history unfolded. Ahman Green's 98-yard bolt to the end zone drew admiration from the Hall of Fame quarterback.

"By the time I finished my fake and turned to look, Ahman was crossing the 50," Favre marveled.

The long-distance sprint was the coup de grâce in Green Bay's 31-3 win over the Denver Broncos in 2003. It enabled the running back to set the franchise single-game rushing record with an outlay of 218 yards.

More importantly, the win – with an assist from the Cardinals, who stunned the Minnesota Vikings on the last play in Arizona – allowed Green Bay (10-6) into the playoffs. The Packers, and not Minnesota (9-7), advanced to the postseason.

"The biggest thing is the win," Green said after his record-setting afternoon. "None of this other stuff matters at all. I don't think anybody would have cared about anything any of us did if we didn't make the playoffs."

Throughout his eight-year Packers career (2000-06, 2009), Green was a threat to go the distance. Yards came quickly and in bunches. Green, the team's all-time leading rusher with 8,322 yards, also holds the team record for runs of 20 or more yards with 53. That's one more than runner-up Jim Taylor.

Pick any multiple of 10 beyond that, and Green is No. 1. Most runs of 30 or more yards? Green with 26. Forty or more? Green with 12.

Go ahead. Run out the string. Green is tops with eight runs of 50 or more yards, eight of 60, four of 70, three of 80, and two of 90 or more yards.

Ahman Green (30) lowers the boom on Arizona Cardinals linebacker Gerald Hayes. (Chip Manthey photo)

In the open field, this back was a sight to behold.

Obtained in trade with Seattle, Green emerged as the Packers' leading rusher in his first year with the team. He rushed for more than 1,000 yards for five straight seasons (2000-04).

His 98-yard excursion, which broke Andy Uram's team record of 97, was a fourth-quarter dash. No surprise there, as Green treated that stanza as any other: a time to advance the ball.

Green is the Packers' all-time fourth-quarter rushing leader. He gained 1,787 yards on 394 attempts (4.54 average).

He led the team in fourth-quarter rushing six times (2000-04, 2006). He broke Dorsey Levens's 1997 single-season record of 457 fourth-quarter yards with a haul of 488 in 2003. The last 98, of course, came with a bang against the Broncos.

Of all who toiled in the backfield for the Packers, Green worked the fourth quarter with the greatest regularity. He had at least one carry there in 92 of the 104 regular-season games in which he played (88.5 percent).

His propensity to pick up yards in chunks carried over into the late going as well. He had more fourth-quarter runs of 10 or more yards (42) than any player in team history.

It was fitting, then, that Green's last carry as a Packer came in the fourth quarter and was a gain of more than 10 yards. With the two-minute warning approaching in the 2009 finale in Arizona, Green zipped for 14 and a first down. His burst allowed quarterback Matt Flynn to follow with three kneel downs to close out a 33-7 triumph over the Cardinals.

Fourth-Quarter Rushing

Career
Packers who rushed for more than 1,000 yards in the fourth quarter.

Yards	Player	Att.	Avg.	LG	TD
1,787	Ahman Green	394	4.54	t98	14
1,652	Jim Taylor	397	4.16	43	25
1,164	Dorsey Levens	267	4.36	50	10
1,106	John Brockington	279	3.96	33	7

Season
Packers who rushed for more than 300 fourth-quarter yards in a season.

Yards	Player, Year	Att.	Avg.	LG	TD
488	Ahman Green, 2003	77	6.34	t98	6
457	Dorsey Levens, 1997	98	4.66	39	4
346	Ryan Grant, 2009	73	4.74	37	1
331	Jim Taylor, 1962	57	5.81	t37	6
328	Ahman Green, 2000	60	5.47	t39	2
313	Ahman Green, 2006	63	4.97	t70	1

Game
Packers who rushed for more than 80 yards in the fourth quarter of a game.

Yards	Player, Date	Att.	Avg.	LG	TD
108	Breezy Reid, Oct. 31, 1953	5	21.60	t38	1
98	Cecil Isbell, Nov. 10, 1940	9	10.89	53	0
98	Ahman Green, Dec. 28, 2003	1	98.00	t98	1
91	Dorsey Levens, Nov. 23, 1997	13	7.00	30	1
90	Tom Moore, Oct. 22, 1961	5	18.00	69	0
86	De'Mond Parker, Dec. 5, 1999	13	6.62	t21	2
83	Jim Taylor, Dec. 10, 1960	11	7.55	25	0

Fourth-Quarter Receiving

Career
Packers who caught more than 135 fourth-quarter passes.

No.	Player	Yards	Avg.	LG	TD
179	Donald Driver	2,337	13.06	t84	14
167	Sterling Sharpe	2,490	14.91	t76	20
137	James Lofton	2,462	17.97	t74	16
136	Jordy Nelson	1,892	13.91	t84	16

Season
Packers who caught 25 or more fourth-quarter passes in a season.

No.	Player, Year	Yards	Avg.	LG	TD
32	Davante Adams, 2018	461	14.41	57	3
30	Sterling Sharpe, 1992	445	14.83	42	3
30	Donald Driver, 2004	415	13.83	39	4
28	Sterling Sharpe, 1989	437	15.61	t55	6
28	Sterling Sharpe, 1993	355	12.68	54	2
27	Bill Schroeder, 1999	417	15.44	42	1
26	Javon Walker, 2004	287	11.04	31	2
25	Harry Sydney, 1992	184	7.36	15	0
25	Davante Adams, 2017	325	13.00	42	4

Game
Packers who caught more than five fourth-quarter passes in a game.

No.	Player, Date	Yards	Avg.	LG	TD
8	Bob Mann, Dec. 16, 1951	49	6.13	14	0
6	Don Hutson, Nov. 15, 1942	69	11.50	20	1
6	Sterling Sharpe, Oct. 22, 1989	67	11.17	t22	2
6	William Henderson, Dec. 7, 1998	36	6.00	15	0
6	Terry Glenn, Sept. 15, 2002	48	8.00	12	0
6	Javon Walker, Oct. 11, 2004	69	11.50	22	1
6	Donald Driver, Nov. 21, 2004	82	13.67	t24	1
6	Eddie Lacy, Nov. 24, 2013	48	8.00	16	0

4th Quarter Receiving
Donald Driver
1999 - 2012

Donald Driver holds the Packers' record for most fourth-quarter receptions with 179. (Photo courtesy of the Green Bay Press-Gazette)

Call him the Centennial Light of Packers receivers.

Donald Driver was longevity personified. A fan favorite, he played nearly a decade and a half at a position where losing a step to age can result in losing playing time to younger, faster athletes.

Driver seemed to go on forever, and his smile could brighten any playing field. The memory of him tracking down passes will not dim any time soon.

Neither will the Centennial Light. Located in Livermore, California, the world's longest-lasting light bulb has been burning since 1901.

Driver played more seasons (14) and in more games (205) than any receiver in team history. The ageless wonder caught more passes after turning 30 than he did when he was in his twenties.

The numbers are impressive. Driver surpassed 1,000 yards receiving six times (2004-09). He caught 50 or more passes in a team-record nine seasons (2002-2010).

Driver accomplished this despite being primarily a back-up during his first three seasons. By the time he became a full-time starter in 2002, he was already 27 years old.

"I walked in here in '99, no one thought a seventh-round draft pick, a high jumper from Alcorn State, was going to make the team. I proved them wrong," Driver said prior to the 2012 season, his last. "As time winds down, you have one bad year, people go, 'It's over for him,' and then you prove 'em wrong again. I'm 37, everybody thinks I'm done. I'll prove 'em wrong again."

Age served to motivate. It had become just another number.

In his twenties, Driver caught 243 passes for 3,413 yards and 23 touchdowns. In his thirties: 500 receptions for 6,724 yards and 38 scores.

His final reception was a 12-yarder on third down that helped set up the Packers' first score in a 24-20 win over the Detroit Lions in November 2012. Driver was 37 years, nine months and 16 days old when he accepted that pass from Aaron Rodgers.

Driver caught more fourth-quarter passes (179) than any Packers player. He caught at least one in a team-record 107 games.

He accumulated more than 20 fourth-quarter catches four times (2004, 2006-08). He led the team in that department in each of those seasons.

Donald Driver takes part in a practice session held at old City Stadium in the summer of 2007. (Eric Goska photo)

Driver was more productive in his thirties in the fourth quarter – 115 catches for 1,405 yards – than he was in his twenties – 64 for 933. Five of his 14 fourth-quarter touchdown catches came after he turned 36.

Double D was most productive in 2004. His 30 catches for 415 yards and four touchdowns were all career bests.

That season, he helped Green Bay overcome a slow start. The team was in danger of missing the playoffs after losing four of its first five games.

With nine games played, the Packers (5-4) were tied with the Minnesota Vikings for first place in the NFC North Division. Next in line: a Sunday night matchup with the Houston Texans (4-5) in the first-ever meeting between the two teams.

Down 13-3 after three quarters, Green Bay opened the floodgates with 210 fourth-quarter yards. Driver, playing in his first professional game in his hometown of Houston, chipped in 82 on six receptions.

Green Bay scored on three of its last four possessions. Driver had at least one catch on all four advances.

His 24-yard TD grab pulled the Packers to within 13-10 with 12 minutes, 28 seconds remaining. His 15-yarder set up Ryan Longwell's game-tying 39-yard field goal with 7:55 to play. And his sideline, 12-yard effort with four seconds left preceded Longwell's 46-yard game-winner as time expired.

"Driver was huge in the second half," left guard Mike Wahle said. "He really bailed us out."

On Christmas Eve 2004, Driver snared five passes for 60 yards and a score in the last eight minutes of Green Bay's 34-31 victory over the Vikings. Among that haul was a 3-yarder on fourth down that tied the score at 31, and two others that went for 25 yards on the game-winning advance, capped by Longwell's 20-yard, walk-off field goal.

"We're always confident," Driver said of the final drive. "We knew we could score."

Those late-season wins against Houston and Minnesota occurred on the road. A team-record 107 of Driver's fourth-quarter catches came in away games.

The Packers were 3-0 in games in which Driver caught five or more fourth-quarter passes. Driver snagged five against the New York Giants, including a 10-yard score, in Green Bay's 35-13 victory on September 16, 2007.

Driver went on a scoring spree of sorts late in his career. Five of his last 10 fourth-quarter receptions resulted in touchdowns, and Green Bay went 8-1 in those games.

Young at Heart

Packers who caught 100 or more passes after turning 30 years of age.

Player, Years	No.	Yards	Avg.	LG	TD
Donald Driver, 2005-2012	500	6,724	13.45	t82	38
Carroll Dale, 1968-1972	183	3,426	18.72	t89	21
Don Hutson, 1943-1945	152	2,476	16.29	t79	29
Jordy Nelson, 2016-2017	150	1,739	11.59	60	20
William Henderson, 2001-2006	147	1,140	7.76	t38	9
Max McGee, 1962-1967	136	2,439	17.93	64	17
Boyd Dowler, 1967-1969	113	1,760	15.58	t72	13

Fourth-Quarter Passing

Career
Packers who threw for 3,400 or more fourth-quarter yards in their career.

Name	Att	Com	Yds	TD	HI	Rate
Brett Favre	2,064	1,246	14,115	98	90	78.54
Aaron Rodgers	1,293	818	10,243	88	26	103.30
Bart Starr	717	424	5,845	40	36	83.01
Lynn Dickey	722	392	5,284	34	40	70.44
Don Majkowski	476	274	3,448	20	20	76.73

Season
Packers who threw for 1,000 or more fourth-quarter yards in a season.

Name, Season	Att	Com	Yds	TD	HI	Rate
Don Majkowski, 1989	181	108	1,424	10	5	91.49
Aaron Rodgers, 2018	176	106	1,408	6	1	94.60
Brett Favre, 1999	177	106	1,347	6	6	80.87
Lynn Dickey, 1983	129	75	1,190	7	8	81.22
Aaron Rodgers, 2015	158	93	1,140	10	4	91.75
Aaron Rodgers, 2016	135	88	1,118	12	2	114.37
Aaron Rodgers, 2008	143	87	1,063	8	5	87.84

Game
Packers who threw for 165 or more fourth-quarter yards in a game.

Name, Date	Att	Com	Yds	TD	HI	Rate
Babe Parilli, Oct. 19, 1958	10	7	219	2	1	112.50
Aaron Rodgers, Sept. 9, 2018	12	9	212	3	0	156.25
Brett Favre, Jan. 2, 2000	12	10	191	1	0	146.53
Brett Favre, Sept. 18, 2005	24	18	190	2	0	125.35
Bobby Thomason, Oct. 28, 1951	13	11	188	3	0	158.33
Brett Favre, Nov. 21, 2004	22	15	185	1	1	90.15
Aaron Rodgers, Nov. 15, 2016	29	17	185	2	0	100.50
Randy Wright, Oct. 26, 1986	21	12	182	0	2	46.23
Brett Favre, Oct. 1, 2000	22	14	172	2	0	117.99
Don Majkowski, Sept. 17, 1989	12	10	170	2	0	158.33
Tobin Rote, Nov. 22, 1956	17	11	166	2	0	135.91
Aaron Rodgers, Jan. 3, 2016	21	13	166	1	1	82.64
Aaron Rodgers, Oct. 7, 2018	16	11	166	1	0	123.44
Bart Starr, Sept. 17, 1967	7	4	165	0	0	101.79

4th Quarter Passing

Don Majkowski
1987 - 1992

Don Majkowski set a Packers record for fourth-quarter passing yards in 1989. (Photo courtesy of the Green Bay Press-Gazette)

The 1989 season had more twists and turns than a riveting novel. Only the final chapter disappointed.

The Packers closed out their seventh decade with panache. Equal parts style and substance, this 10-6 team had a flair for the dramatic.

Seven times the Pack came from behind to win. Four times it prevailed by a single point. The team even tamed the Chicago Bears twice in the same season for the first time in eight years.

This rollercoaster ride was as welcome as it was unexpected. A year earlier, first-year head coach Lindy Infante's team had finished 4-12. That aggregation was shut out three times and failed to score 10 points on three other occasions.

Quarterbacks Don Majkowski (67.8 rating) and Randy Wright (59.0) took turns at the controls. Wright was 1-6 as a starter; Majkowski was 3-6.

As training camp opened, Infante said: "I don't want to label it (QB) as the No. 1 need on this football team, but somebody has to step forward. Whether that means somebody we have or somebody who will come in the future, someone has to make a statement that he's the guy to take us to the Promised Land."

Speculation was the Packers might select UCLA quarterback Troy Aikman with the second pick in the draft. If not, Washington State's Timm Rosenbach or Miami's Steve Walsh might become available in the supplemental draft.

Turns out, those three weren't needed. For one year at least, Majkowski morphed into the "Majik" man, and his play was good enough to spark a six-game turnaround.

Majkowski led the league with 4,318 passing yards. His 27 touchdowns ranked third behind Buffalo's Jim Kelly (29) and Cincinnati's Boomer Esiason (28). He passed for more than 300 yards six times.

The quarterback from Virginia attempted all but one of Green Bay's 600 passes. At the time, his 599 throws were the sixth most by an NFL player in one season.

Majkowski was especially effective in the fourth quarter. His rating there (91.5) was higher than what he earned in the first (88.9), second (62.6) or third (88.1) quarters.

The 1,454 yards he passed for in that period in 1989 remain the team record. His 10 fourth-quarter TD passes tied him with Joe Montana for most in the league.

Green Bay fell behind 11 times in the fourth quarter. It rallied for victory in five of those contests.

With that in mind, Majkowski's work in 1989 can be divided into three parts. The numbers that correspond with each attest to the never-say-die nature of this collection of overachievers.

- Green Bay posted five wins in which it never trailed in the fourth quarter. In the final 15 minutes of those games, Majkowski completed 23 of 42 passes for 245 yards with a touchdown and two interceptions. That was good for a 60.1 rating, which suggests Majkowski did little down the stretch when his team was in control after three quarters.

- The Packers lost six of the 11 games in which they trailed in the fourth quarter. Majkowski completed 47 of 81 passes for 555 yards, three touchdowns and two interceptions. Needing to rally appeared to elevate the level of his play as his rating in these games (81.0) was more than 20 points better than in the games in which Green Bay did not trail in the fourth quarter.

- Finally, the Green and Gold erased fourth-quarter deficits to win five times. In fueling those comebacks, Majkowski was darn near unstoppable, compiling a rating of 128.6 on 39 completions in 59 attempts for 631 yards, six touchdowns and one interception.

Twice Green Bay rose up after being down 10 points or more in the fourth quarter. In arrears 31-21 to the New Orleans Saints, Majkowski completed a pair of touchdowns to tight end Ed West to register a 35-34 win. Behind 21-6 against the Atlanta Falcons, Majkowski hit on five of seven for 90 yards and a score (Herman Fontenot) to notch a 23-21 victory.

The Packers also rallied from six, three and six back to topple the Chicago Bears (14-13), Minnesota Vikings (20-19) and Tampa Bay Buccaneers (17-16). Majkowski fired a fourth-quarter TD pass in each of those games with the most memorable being a 14-yarder to Sterling Sharpe against Chicago that was allowed only after replay review.

"Never, never, never, never, never – NO, NEVER – count the '89 Green Bay Packers out of a football game," *Green Bay Press-Gazette* beat reporter Bob McGinn wrote after Chris Jacke kicked Tampa Bay to the curb with a walk-off, 47-yard field goal on December 3.

In that game, Green Bay appeared dead after Majkowski threw a fourth-down incompletion with 47 seconds left. But umpire Ed Fiffick flagged defensive tackle Shawn Lee for illegal hands to the face on the play, and given new life, Majkowski completed three of six passes to set up Jacke's boot.

The Packers closed out the regular season with wins at Chicago (40-28) and Dallas (20-10).

"(Majkowski) is everything to that team," Bears safety David Tate said. "They play over their heads, and this is what happens."

Despite a 10-6 record, Green Bay needed help to get into the playoffs. The Los Angeles Rams and Philadelphia Eagles had locked up the two NFC wild card spots, so winning the Central Division title was the Packers' last chance. For that to happen, the Bengals would have to defeat the Vikings on Christmas night.

A group of players gathered at the home of linebacker Brian Noble to watch Minnesota host Cincinnati in the season's final regular-season game. But when the Vikings prevailed 29-21, they matched Green Bay's 10-6 record and were awarded the division title because of a better division record (6-2 vs. 5-3) than the Packers.

"I'm a big fan of Don Majkowski," Esiason said after his Bengals lost. "I would have loved to have given him the opportunity to go to the playoffs."

Majkowski finished his career with the Indianapolis Colts (1993-94) and Detroit Lions (1995-96). His lone playoff appearance came in a 58-37 loss to the Eagles on December 30, 1995.

Fourth-Quarter Scoring

Career
Packers who scored more than 150 fourth-quarter points in their career.

Points	Name	TDs	PAT	FG
400	Mason Crosby	0	133-138	89-111
282	Ryan Longwell	0	102-102	60-68
214	Paul Hornung	20	58-59	12-31
212	Don Hutson	27	43-45	2-6
183	Chris Jacke	0	81-83	34-43
162	Jim Taylor	27	0-0	0-0

Season
Packers who scored 42 or more points in the fourth quarter of one season.

Points	Name, Season	TDs	PAT	FG
76	Paul Hornung, 1960	9	16-16	2-4
46	Mason Crosby, 2008	0	16-16	10-12
43	Mason Crosby, 2007	0	10-10	11-13
42	Don Hutson, 1943	5	9-9	1-1
42	Jim Taylor, 1961	7	0-0	0-0
42	Sterling Sharpe, 1989	7	0-0	0-0
42	Ahman Green, 2003	7	0-0	0-0

Game
Packers who scored more than 12 points in the fourth quarter of a game.

Points	Name, Date	TDs	PAT	FG
18	Hal Van Every, Nov. 23, 1941	3	0-0	0-0
14	Don Hutson, Dec. 5, 1943	2	2-2	0-0
14	Paul Hornung, Oct. 2, 1960	2	2-2	0-0
13	Andy Uram, Nov. 24, 1940	2	1-1	0-0
13	Andy Uram, Nov. 1, 1942	2	1-1	0-0

4th Quarter Scoring

Paul Hornung
1957 - 1962, 1964-1966

Paul Hornung leaps across the goal line during the Packers' 41-14 pounding of the San Francisco 49ers in 1960. (Photo courtesy of the Green Bay Press-Gazette)

Had the season been longer, Paul Hornung might have doubled up Bobby Walston. In 1960, Hornung produced points with breakneck speed. He went from zero to 100 faster than any player in history.

He set Packers and NFL records alike. He left everybody in his wake.

Hornung had led the league in scoring before. He did so for the first time in 1959 with 94 points.

One year later, he outdid himself. With Green Bay on its way to a championship game appearance for the first time in 16 years, Hornung amassed an NFL-record 176 points.

Hornung's total broke Don Hutson's previous record of 138. Hornung's 176 points were more than the combined total produced by everyone else on the team that year, a group that included Jim Taylor, Max McGee and Boyd Dowler – no strangers to the end zone themselves.

For all that Hornung accomplished in his career as runner, passer, and receiver, it is this scoring spree that has never been surpassed. Yes, LaDainian Tomlinson charged to 186 points in 2006 (16-game season), but Hornung's average of 14.7 points per game has never been seriously threatened.

Early on, there was no indication something special was afoot. After three weeks, Taylor paced all scorers with 30 points. Hornung was second with 29.

By late October, that changed. Hornung's 23-point performance in a 41-14 dismantling of the San Francisco 49ers catapulted him to the fore. Once there, he never wavered. In fact, the distance between first and second only widened.

Statistics released the week of October 26 showed Hornung as the NFL's leading scorer with 52 points. Walston, the talented end who doubled as kicker for the Philadelphia Eagles, was next with 51.

If Walston, who led the league in scoring in 1954 with 114 points, thought he might again be No. 1, he was sadly mistaken.

At the season's halfway point, Hornung had 83 points. Walston was 22 points back with 61.

When Hornung hit 100 – doing so in a record-low seven games – Walston had 74. When Hornung jumped to 119, Walston baby-stepped to 79.

The gap between the two players went from 40 to 43 to 58 to 68. When the final accounting took place, Walston's 105 points – enough to have led the league most years – came up 71 short of Hornung's haul.

Given more time, Hornung might have scored twice as many points as Walston.

Hornung broke Hutson's single-season record in a 41-13 triumph over the Chicago Bears. He tallied 23 points at Wrigley Field that first Sunday in December.

"You don't think that much about records," Hornung said after the game which, coupled with Detroit's win over Baltimore, sent Green Bay into a three-way tie for first place in the Western Division. "Somebody will come along and break this one."

In 1960, Hornung scored a league-high 15 TDs: 13 rushing and two receiving. He was perfect on 41 extra-point tries and converted 15 of 28 field goal attempts.

He could, and perhaps should, have had more. Seven of his misses came from distances of less than 35 yards.

Hornung's impressive output in 1960 included a record-setting fourth quarter as well. Walston, again, played second fiddle.

Green Bay's prized halfback scored 76 points in the fourth, a team record. It was far more that his totals in the first (29), second (32) and third periods (39).

Hornung scored nine fourth-quarter touchdowns, eight on the ground. He kicked 16 extra points and connected on two of four field goal attempts.

A season-high 14-point outing against the Detroit Lions in early October got him rolling. He also scored 10 points in fourth quarters in Baltimore and in San Francisco.

Walston finished second in the NFL in fourth-quarter scoring with 52 points.

Amazingly, the Packers didn't need any of Hornung's fourth-quarter points. Had they vanished, Green Bay still would have met the Eagles for all the marbles.

Even in the championship game, Walston couldn't match Hornung. Walston came away with five points to Hornung's six.

That turn of events was meaningless to Hornung. His team lost 17-13 at Franklin Field that day.

Hornung likely was more concerned with the three points he didn't get. He blew a 14-yard chip shot at the end of the first half that would have pulled Green Bay to within one point (10-9) of the Eagles. That miss and the three-point loss to Philadelphia made for a bitter ending to a season loaded with promise and points.

Super(fluous) Scoring

Paul Hornung scored 76 points in the fourth quarter in 1960. It is the most points scored by any Packers player in any quarter of any season.

Amazingly, Green Bay didn't need any of those 76 points. Had they vanished and all else remained the same, the Packers still would have finished 8-4 and met the Philadelphia Eagles in the championship game.

The game-by-game regular-season results below include the points Hornung tallied in the fourth quarter and what the Packers' score would have been without them.

(M) = game played in Milwaukee

Date		PF	Opponent	PA	Hornung's 4th Quarter				Without Hornung	
					TD	FG	XP	Total	PF	Result
9-25	L	14	Bears	17	0	0	0	0	14	L
10-2	W	28	Lions	9	2	0	2	14	14	W
10-9	W	35	Colts	21	0	0	3	3	32	W
10-23	W	41	49ers (M)	14	1	0	2	8	33	W
10-30	W	19	at Steelers	13	0	0	1	1	18	W
11-6	L	24	at Colts	38	1	1	1	10	14	L
11-13	W	41	Cowboys	7	1	0	1	7	34	W
11-20	L	31	Rams (M)	33	1	0	2	8	23	L
11-24	L	10	at Lions	23	0	0	0	0	10	L
12-4	W	41	at Bears	13	1	0	2	8	33	W
12-10	W	13	at 49ers	0	1	1	1	10	3	W
12-17	W	35	at Rams	21	1	0	1	7	28	W
		332		209	9	2	16	76	256	

Lasting Impressions
Final Plays

Wide receiver Sterling Sharpe is the Packers' all-time leading receiver on the team's final play, including the winning touchdown in one of the most famous games in Packers-Bears history. (Photo courtesy of the Green Bay Press-Gazette)

November 5, 1989

The Bears referenced the game with an asterisk.

The Packers celebrated with an exclamation point.

Regardless of what side you come down on, Green Bay's 14-13 triumph over Chicago on November 5, 1989, will always be the Instant Replay game. The deciding play was reviewed repeatedly that afternoon, and it resurfaces again and again as the history of the team gets imparted to each new generation of fans.

To comprehend the sheer joy that erupted that afternoon in Lambeau Field requires at least a passing understanding of the misery the Packers had endured at the hands of the Bears. For four straight years, Chicago ruled the rivalry, always coming out on top no matter how agonizingly close Green Bay came to victory.

In 1985, Walter Payton's 27-yard, fourth-quarter run torpedoed the Packers 16-10. In 1986 and 1987, Kevin Butler supplied last-minute, game-winning field goals of 32 and 52 yards, the latter coming as time expired.

Those defeats came on Forrest Gregg's watch. Lindy Infante replaced Gregg as Packers head coach in 1988, and the losing continued.

In 1988, the team was clubbed 24-6 and 16-0. The Green and Gold was outgained by more than 300 yards in the two games combined, and it failed to score on any of its last 21 possessions against the Bears that year.

Jump ahead to 1989, and the first meeting between the two was again looking bleak for the Packers. Trailing 13-7 with 41 seconds remaining, the club faced fourth-and-goal from the Bears' 14-yard line.

Quarterback Don Majkowski lined up in the shotgun. Running back Herman Fontenot joined him in the backfield.

Four receivers spread the field: Perry Kemp and Aubrey Matthews aligned to Majkowski's right, and Jeff Query and Sterling Sharpe took up positions to his left.

At the snap, Majkowski retreated. Feeling pressure, he stepped up in the pocket then drifted to his right.

By then, Trace Armstrong had disengaged from tackle Tony Mandarich. The defensive end headed toward Majkowski, and the two approached the Packers' sideline.

Scanning the end zone while gliding ever closer to the line of scrimmage, Majkowski finally pulled the trigger. Replays showed his foot appeared to be on the 15-yard stripe when he launched the throw.

The ball traveled toward a relatively small window that had opened between defensive back Markus Paul and linebacker Mike Singletary. Before that gap could close, Sterling Sharpe accepted Majkowski's pass about two yards deep in the end zone. He absorbed a hit from defensive back Dave Duerson just before field judge Bernie Kukar raised his arms to signal touchdown.

"I was hoping Don saw me," said Sharpe. "I was in the end zone and I was just praying nobody was behind me. Don saw me at the last second and threw a strike."

Majkowski jumped into the arms of backup quarterback Blair Kiel. Sharpe, who had been a nonfactor for 59 minutes (one catch), shared a group hug with Query, Kemp and Matthews. Teammates pounded their backs.

If ever there was a time to celebrate, this was it. Or was it?

Referee Jim Dooley turned on his microphone to announce a penalty. Line judge Jim Quirk had thrown a flag for an illegal forward pass. In the eyes of the officials, Majkowski had released the ball beyond the line of scrimmage.

The infraction, of course, carried with it loss of down. If the call stood, it would be Bears' ball with 32 seconds left.

From his perch in level 3 of the press box, Bill Parkinson examined and re-examined the throw. The replay official took his time – more than four minutes – before handing down his verdict.

"After further review, we have a reversal: touchdown." Dooley intoned from the field.

Raw emotion electrified the stadium. The outpouring only intensified after Chris Jacke tacked on the extra point.

"I still don't like (instant replay). I still think it takes a lot away from the game," Sharpe said. "Today, I guess, I'll have to live with it and tell everybody it's the greatest thing since ice water."

"What's the guy's (instant replay official) name?" Packers linebacker Brian Noble asked. "I'd like to send him a bottle of champagne."

Three decades later, echoes of Majkowski-to-Sharpe continue to reverberate. The

Don Majkowski celebrates after his touchdown pass to Sterling Sharpe is ruled good by the replay official in the Instant Replay Game against the Chicago Bears in 1989 at Lambeau Field. (Photo courtesy of the Green Bay Press-Gazette)

moment created a lasting impression.

The Packers have run tens of thousands of offensive plays over the years. Only the team's final offensive play qualifies as a lasting impression.

Sharpe's 14-yard TD catch was the final snap for Green Bay in beating the Bears. Chicago ran out the clock in a futile attempt to get into field goal range.

The Packers have run more than 1,350 final plays since their first league game against the Minneapolis Marines in 1921. The type and distance covered can be determined for all but roughly 30 of those snaps.

Sharpe is the team's top touchdown receiver with six. Tony Canadeo is the team's top touchdown rusher with six.

A total of 153 touchdowns – 65 rushing and 88 receiving – were scored on final plays. Twenty-five were game-winners.

Antonio Freeman twisted free for the longest gain (84 yards) in the 1998 opener against the Detroit Lions. At the other end of the spectrum, Irv Comp (1944) and Aaron Rodgers (2018) were set back 18 yards on final plays against the Card-Pitt (Carpets, a combined team of the Chicago Cardinals and Pittsburgh Steelers during World War II) and Bears, respectively.

Sharpe also made a lasting impression in the postseason. He scored on a 29-yard pass from Brett Favre in the Packers' 27-17 loss in Dallas on January 16, 1994.

That came eight days after he nearly had another. In Detroit, he reeled in a 40-yard bomb with 55 seconds to go.

The play, however, was not Green Bay's last. The Packers got the ball back with 25 seconds remaining, and Favre – the author of that long heave – took a knee to close out a 28-24 win.

In 1990, Ditka asked that an asterisk appear next to the score of the first Packers-Bears game of 1989 in the team's media guide. The symbol made reference to a simple three-word notation at the bottom of the page: "Instant replay game."

Final Plays

Longest Final Plays

Yds.	Play	Date	Opponent
84	Antonio Freeman pass from Brett Favre	Sept. 6, 1998	Lions
82	Greg Jennings pass from Brett Favre	Oct. 29, 2007	Broncos
76	Najeh Davenport run	Oct. 19, 2003	Rams
75	Bill Howton pass from Babe Parilli	Oct. 27, 1957	Colts
61	Richard Rodgers pass from Aaron Rodgers	Dec. 3, 2015	Lions
56	Walter Stanley pass from Don Majkowski	Oct. 2, 1988	Buccaneers
54	Equanimeous St. Brown pass from Aaron Rodgers	Oct. 7, 2018	Lions

Leading Rushers

Name	Att.	Yards	Avg.	LG	TD
Najeh Davenport	4	118	29.50	t76	2
Tony Canadeo	15	108	7.20	t35	6
Joe Laws	10	55	5.50	17	1
Lou Brock	5	51	10.20	42	1
Lamar McHan	5	50	10.00	35	1

Leading Receivers

Name	No.	Yards	Avg.	LG	TD
Sterling Sharpe	9	138	15.33	34	6
Antonio Freeman	6	206	34.33	t84	5
James Lofton	6	78	13.00	29	1
Lavvie Dilweg	5	101	20.20	36	2
Rich McGeorge	5	84	16.80	40	2
Paul Coffman	5	40	8.00	15	2

Leading Passers

Name	Att.	Com.	Yards	TD	HI
Brett Favre	70	30	525	18	15
Aaron Rodgers	48	24	351	9	3
Bart Starr	41	19	213	7	12
Babe Parilli	13	8	193	4	3
Don Majkowski	24	10	193	4	5
Lynn Dickey	31	15	143	4	8

OT - Other Topics

Davante Adams takes a Brett Hundley pass 25 yards for the winning score in Green Bay's 27-21 overtime win against the Cleveland Browns in 2017. (Photo courtesy of the Green Bay Press-Gazette)

Down and Distant

Jerry Kramer's 1961 season ended with an ankle injury on the same day the Packers faced a third-and-unlikely situation against the Minnesota Vikings. (Photo courtesy of the Green Bay Press-Gazette)

Bart Starr had never been in such a situation.

As Starr surveyed the Minnesota Vikings' defense on a late October afternoon in 1961, it's possible he couldn't spot the first-down marker. It stood 53 yards downfield in the rain and gloom of Milwaukee's County Stadium.

Third-and-53. Might as well have been third-and-forever.

What play does one dial up when more than half the length of a football field is needed for a fresh set of downs? What play is designed to cover that distance?

"Starr looked over at me, and I ducked," Packers coach Vince Lombardi joked to reporters afterward. "I didn't know what to tell him."

With no guidance from the sidelines, the resourceful quarterback took matters into his own hands: he threw short to Ron Kramer. The big tight end gained nine yards, 44 short of what was needed, and the Packers punted.

Fortunately for Green Bay, the play had little impact on the outcome. Starr and the Packers prevailed over the Vikings – an expansion team that season – by a 28-10 score.

Plays requiring more than 10 yards for a first down show up virtually every Sunday. Rare is the team that can avoid a miscue that doesn't put them in a down-and-distant situation.

Circumstances involving length can be intriguing for two reasons: the frustrating, sometimes comedic events that send a team into reverse, and the play or plays chosen to atone for those blunders.

In the case of Lombardi's Packers, twice the team was called for holding. Starr was then sacked by defensive tackle Ed Culpepper.

Boom! Just like that, a drive went from doable to doubtful.

The 53 yards called for to move the chains that fall day is the greatest distance Green Bay has faced on any down in which it did not punt or attempt a field goal since 1954. It is likely a team record.

On average, the Packers encounter lengthy downs about seven times a game. The team typically chooses to pass more often than run when those situations arise.

Green Bay has been down and distant-free just six times in 970 regular-season games from 1954 through 2018. On another 18 occasions, it encountered one such play.

More common are those games in which the team backs up and often. Green Bay faced 12 or more down-and-distant plays in 91 games from 1954-2018. That number exceeded 14 on 16 occasions.

Green Bay bottomed out on October 24, 1976, in Oakland. A team-record 23 of its 68 offensive plays demanded more than 10 yards for a first down. This was due in part to seven holding penalties, four quarterback sacks, and three negative running plays.

The Packers moved the chains on just two of those 23 distant downs. Lynn Dickey scrambled for 12 yards in the closing seconds, and he connected with wide receiver Steve Odom for 21 in the second quarter.

In the end, being repeatedly asked to generate big yardage was too much to ask. Green Bay lost 18-14 to the Raiders, who faced 11 distant plays that afternoon.

Nearly six years after coming up short on third-and-53 against the Vikings, Starr was again at the controls when the offense converted a third-and-39 against the Detroit Lions in the 1967 season opener. That distance is the longest the team has overcome to earn a fresh set of downs.

With Detroit ahead 17-7 early in the fourth quarter, Starr flipped a screen pass to Jim Grabowski. Aided by a block from tight end Marv Fleming, the fullback rumbled to the 2-yard line, where rookie cornerback Lem Barney brought him down.

Elijah Pitts scored on the next play. Don Chandler then added a field goal, but

Green Bay had to settle for a 17-17 tie with the Lions, who were two-touchdown underdogs.

Joe Falls of the *Detroit Free Press* wrote: "What happened is that Bart Starr recovered from a horrendous first half and shocked the Lions with some of the most fantastic third-down plays ever seen in any pro game."

Starr, who threw four first-half interceptions, hit Pitts for an 84-yard gain on third-and-19 to set up Chandler's kick. He also connected with Boyd Dowler for 13 to get to the Detroit 38 on third-and-10, but time ran out before the big end could get out of bounds.

Back 40

The 12 plays in which the Packers needed 40 or more yards for a first down.

Date	Down	Dist	Play	Opponent
Nov. 29, 1961	3rd	53	Bart Starr pass Ron Kramer for 9	Vikings
Dec. 9, 1967	3rd	45	Bart Starr run for 23	Rams
Oct. 29, 1961	2nd	42	Bart Starr sacked for loss of 11	Vikings
Nov. 1, 1970	2nd	42	Donny Anderson run for 13	49ers
Nov. 9, 1958	3rd	41	Bart Starr run for 4	Bears
Oct. 12, 1970	3rd	41	Bart Starr pass Carroll Dale for 18	Chargers
Nov. 17, 1937	1st	40	Arnie Herber pass intercepted	Rams
Oct. 3, 1948	3rd	40	Jack Jacobs pass intercepted	Lions
Oct. 4, 1953	2nd	40	Tobin Rote pass incomplete	Bears
Oct. 4, 1953	3rd	40	Tobin Rote run for 14	Bears
Sept. 28, 1958	2nd	40	Bart Starr pass Don McIlhenny for 0	Bears
Sept. 28, 1958	3rd	40	Bart Starr pass incomplete	Bears

Faraway Firsts

The 12 plays in which the Packers earned a first down when more than 25 yards was required.

Date	Down	Dist	Play	Opponent
Sept. 17, 1967	3rd	39	Bart Starr pass Jim Grabowski for 53	Lions
Oct. 10, 1948	3rd	37	Jug Girard pass Nolan Luhn for 40	Cardinals
Oct. 31, 1953	2nd	36	Breezy Reid run for 37	Colts
Oct. 27, 1963	3rd	34	John Roach pass Max McGee for 36	Colts
Oct. 11, 1936	1st	30	Johnny Blood run for 30	Redskins
Dec. 7, 1969	3rd	29	Don Horn pass Dave Hampton for t29	Browns
Nov. 26, 1959	2nd	28	Bart Starr pass Boyd Dowler for 30	Lions
Dec. 17, 1967	1st	27	Bart Starr pass Donny Anderson for 31	Steelers
Dec. 13, 1960	3rd	26	Rick Norton pass John Hilton for t29	Bears
Oct. 4, 1981	3rd	26	Lynn Dickey pass John Jefferson for t26	Giants
Oct. 10, 1999	3rd	26	Brett Favre pass Antonio Freeman for 43	Buccaneers
Sept. 13, 2012	4th	26	Tim Masthay pass Tom Crabtree for t27	Bears

t = touchdown

All-Positive 100s

Ahman Green posted a team-record three all-positive 100-yard rushing days while with the Packers. Here, he glides through a hole against the Minnesota Vikings. (Photo courtesy of the Green Bay Press-Gazette)

Does having a positive attitude make a difference?
One group to ask might be those who have assembled an all-positive, 100-yard rushing day. Though the sample size is small, their answers could be revealing.

An all-positive 100 is not easily attained. It requires a player to amass 100 or more rushing yards while gaining positive yardage on every carry without fumbling.

Check those boxes and you're in.

Running backs have gained 100 yards rushing in a game more than 200 times in Packers history. More than 50 players have reached or exceeded the milestone.

Ten players have produced an all-positive 100 (AP 100). There have been 12 known cases in team annals.

Running backs are marked men. Every carry is a green light for 11 highly motivated athletes to come knock them down. Defenders are always looking to end a play sooner rather than later. Getting tackled at or behind the line of scrimmage is a possibility on any down.

For eight seasons, Ahman Green had a target on his back. Green Bay's all-time leading rusher (8,322 yards) gained more than 1,000 yards six different times (2000-2004, 2006).

His numbers are impressive. The man knew how to attack a defense.

Green piled up 100 or more yards rushing a team-record 33 times. He did so on at least three occasions during each of his 1,000-yard campaigns.

On November 10, 2003, Green carved out 192 yards against the Philadelphia Eagles. On September 9, 2001, he feasted on 157 yards at the expense of the Detroit Lions.

Both were stellar performances, but neither was an AP 100. In each case, Green was dumped for a loss more than once.

Year after year, running backs put up glitzy numbers like those of Green. Yet lurking somewhere in those massive totals is often an excursion or two that gets blown up before it gets started.

Green ran the ball 1,851 times during his Packers' career. As special as he was, going forward sometimes proved impossible.

The four-time Pro Bowl selection gained nothing or was thrown for a loss 310 times while in Green Bay. He was held up most often in 2001 (57) and in 2003 (56).

This lack of positivity did not prevent Green from becoming the only Packer to produce more than one AP 100. The forward-thinking back got there on three occasions, twice in one season (2003).

Green staged his first all-positive, 100-yard outing on October 5, 2003. If it was not his most memorable showing, it certainly was his busiest.

Green carried 27 times against the Seattle Seahawks at Lambeau Field. He produced positive yardage each time and did not fumble.

He wasn't flashy. His long run was 16 yards. Nineteen of his tries garnered four or fewer yards. Only twice did he have gains of more than 10.

But every time he was tackled, he landed beyond the line of scrimmage.

"Right now, he's running with a lot of hunger and patience," said fellow running back Tony Fisher. "And if he keeps running like he is, the rest of this team is just going to follow him."

Green scored two second-quarter rushing touchdowns. He carried at least once on each of Green Bay's eight offensive possessions.

The Packers beat Seattle 35-13. Green led all runners with 118 yards.

Seven times he was held to a single yard. Had any one of those runs been scored as no gain, Green would have been denied an AP 100.

In evaluating the game, *The Milwaukee Journal-Sentinel* reporter Bob McGinn wrote: "Green can take it hard up inside or he can bounce it outside. He is punishing and powerful, but also patient and more elusive than in the past. He isn't fumbling."

The 100-yard effort was Green's third in a season just five games old. He'd finish with 1,883 yards, breaking Jim Taylor's record of 1,474.

Green was drafted in the third round by the Seahawks in 1998. A year later, Mike Holmgren became Seattle's head coach and general manager, and he traded Green to the Packers in 2000.

The running back claimed he wasn't out to prove something to his old team.

"It brought me back to when I transferred high schools and played against my old high school team in Omaha – Central vs. North," Green said. "It's just a game – got to go out there and have fun, stay focused and not get too caught up in the other emotions."

Green's two other AP 100s occurred on December 28, 2003, (20 carries for 218 yards) and October 29, 2006, (21 for 106). Green's 27 rushing attempts against the Seahawks are the most by any Packers player in an all-positive setting.

Andy Uram generated the first AP 100. He ripped off runs of 11 and 97 yards in a 27-20 win over the Chicago Cardinals in 1939.

Tobin Rote became the only quarterback in this illustrious group when he staked out 131 yards on Thanksgiving Day 1951. He had six gains of 10 or more yards and counted on a 1-yard run in the first quarter in a 52-35 loss to the Lions.

Howie Ferguson almost didn't make it. He gained exactly 100 yards in 11 trips in a 37-21 loss to the Washington Redskins in 1958.

Billy Grimes, Breezy Reid, Jim Grabowski, Gerry Ellis, Eddie Lee Ivery, and Ryan Grant also had AP 100s.

Others came close. One fumble prevented Donny Anderson from joining the ranks in 1969. Clarke Hinkle, Jim Taylor, MacArthur Lane, Edgar Bennett, Dorsey Levens, Darick Holmes, and Eddie Lacy came up short because each had a run for no gain. Tony Canadeo, Lew Carpenter, Jessie Clark, Kevin Wilhite, and DeShawn Wynn failed because of a single run for a loss.

Taylor was the only player to be denied on his final attempt. After racking up 121 yards on 14 trips against the Dallas Cowboys in 1960, the fullback was stopped at the line of scrimmage. Larry Hickman then took over for him in the fourth quarter of Green Bay's 41-7 rout.

That's how quickly a bid for an AP 100 can end.

Positively 100

Packers players who gained 100 yards rushing in a game without fumbling, and who did so by earning positive yardage on each of their carries.

Name	Att.	Yards	Date
Andy Uram	2	108	Oct. 8, 1939
Billy Grimes	10	167	Oct. 8, 1950
Tobin Rote	15	131	Nov. 22, 1951
Breezy Reid	9	120	Oct. 31, 1953
Howie Ferguson	11	100	Oct. 19, 1958
Jim Grabowski	21	123	Oct. 22, 1967
Gerry Ellis	15	101	Nov. 23, 1980
Eddie Lee Ivery	9	116	Oct. 28, 1984
Ahman Green	27	118	Oct. 5, 2003
Ahman Green	20	218	Dec. 28, 2003
Ahman Green	21	106	Oct. 29, 2006
Ryan Grant	19	104	Dec. 7, 2008

Fail-Safe 100s

Imagine setting a standard. Then imagine never failing to live up to that ideal.

That, in essence, is the idea behind the fail-safe 100 passer rating.

Quarterbacks who enjoy a fail-safe outing never have their rating fall below 100. You could stop the action at any point in a game, crunch the numbers, and their rating would be triple digits.

Each year, scores of players earn passer ratings of 100 or more in a game. Far less common are those who stay at or above 100 from first pass to last.

In 1984, Lynn Dickey was not looking to become the third player in Packers history to achieve fail-safe status as his team prepared for a late-October meeting with the Detroit Lions. The quarterback and his teammates just wanted a win, any win.

Green Bay had dropped seven straight during Forrest Gregg's first season as Packers head coach. At the halfway mark, the Green and Gold (1-7) had the third-worst record in the NFL behind the winless Buffalo Bills and Houston Oilers.

Even so, Gregg wasn't ready to write off the season. But he wasn't planning on making any sweeping changes to turn the tide, either.

"We've made about all the adjustments we can make with the people that we have," he said. "Those people are just going to have to tighten up their belts."

No changes meant Dickey would get the start. He had been Green Bay's

Lynn Dickey was just the third Packers player to compile a fail-safe 100 passer rating. (Photo courtesy of the Green Bay Press-Gazette)

preferred starter at quarterback since then-head coach Bart Starr had traded for him in April 1976.

At 35, Dickey was nearing the end of his career. His lack of mobility, from numerous injuries suffered over the years, left him susceptible to pressure.

Cecil Isbell (far left) was the first Packers passer to compile a fail-safe 100 passer rating. Here he is on the receiving end of a toss from Arnie Herber against the Washington Redskins at State Fair Park in Milwaukee. (Photo courtesy of the Green Bay Press-Gazette)

Through eight games, Dickey was on pace to be sacked 52 times, which would have been a team record. He also had thrown 12 interceptions, the second-most in the league.

"Until Forrest (Gregg) makes the decision, we've got to go with Lynn because he can win for us," Packers offensive coordinator Bob Schnelker said. "He's capable of having great football games."

If Green Bay were to beat Detroit, it would have to do a better job protecting Dickey. Gregg said as much as game time approached.

"There are keys for us to win Sunday. Our defense must play better than last week (a 30-24 loss to Seattle), and our offense must be able to handle Detroit's front four."

Detroit's front four consisted of ends Michael Cofer and William Gay, and tackles Curtis Green and Doug English. Gay (13.5 sacks) and English (13) had been among the league leaders in sacks in 1983.

The Packers had had little success against the Lions in the early 1980s. They had dropped seven of eight against their rivals from 1980 through 1983.

A solid start is necessary when fashioning a fail-safe 100. The first pass thrown must be a completion and it must yield at least eight yards.

Dickey completed his first nine passes against the Lions. All nine resulted in first downs.

His sixth pass went to Paul Coffman for 20 yards and a touchdown. His ninth throw again found the tight end and Green Bay went up 21-6.

Dickey's passer rating after each of his first five throws was 118.75. It jumped to the maximum 158.3 with his first touchdown toss and it stayed there until an incompletion on his 13th attempt dropped it to 151.4.

Dickey returned to 158.3 one last time with a 21-yard completion to James Lofton on the final drive of the first half. Dickey failed to ascend to that level on any of his final 11 throws despite touchdown strikes to backup offensive lineman Blake Moore and Lofton.

In the 41-9 downing of Detroit, Dickey completed 17 of 25 passes for 248 yards and four touchdowns. His final passer rating was 139.7, but could have been higher had his last three attempts not fallen incomplete.

Detroit's front four failed to sack Dickey. Linebacker Garry Cobb was the only Lion to get to him, and he did so in the third quarter with Green Bay up 35-9.

"I had excellent time to throw," Dickey said. "The Lions have a good defensive front, but I think our line was ready to play. In fact, they've been ready to play for the last four or five weeks."

Having a solid running game also helped. Eddie Lee Ivery rushed for 116 yards on nine carries as the Packers piled up 195 yards on the ground.

Dickey's fail-safe performance was the only one of his career. He became the third Packers passer – Cecil Isbell (2 times) and Bart Starr (3) – to keep his rating in triple digits for an entire game (minimum 20 attempts).

Without Fail

Date	Player	Att.	Com.	Yds.	TD	HI	Final Rate	Low Point
Oct. 26, 1941	Cecil Isbell	21	13	182	3	0	129.4	100.5
Oct. 18, 1942	Cecil Isbell	33	23	277	2	0	115.3	102.1
Nov. 10, 1957	Bart Starr	21	12	179	2	0	117.0	115.2
Dec. 2, 1962	Bart Starr	20	15	260	2	0	150.0	118.8
Nov. 12, 1967	Bart Starr	21	14	249	2	1	118.9	112.9
Oct. 28, 1984	Lynn Dickey	25	17	248	4	0	139.7	118.8
Nov. 13, 1994	Brett Favre	28	20	183	2	0	112.6	100.0
Nov. 12, 1995	Brett Favre	33	25	336	5	0	147.2	111.5
Dec. 16, 1995	Brett Favre	30	21	308	4	0	142.8	118.8
Nov. 10, 2002	Brett Favre	39	26	351	2	0	112.2	102.6
Nov. 28, 2010	Aaron Rodgers	35	26	344	1	0	114.5	100.4
Sept. 25, 2011	Aaron Rodgers	38	28	297	3	1	111.4	100.0
Oct. 23, 2011	Aaron Rodgers	30	24	335	3	0	146.5	112.5
Oct. 21, 2012	Aaron Rodgers	37	30	342	3	0	132.2	100.0
Oct. 27, 2013	Aaron Rodgers	29	24	285	2	0	130.6	100.8
Sept. 28, 2014	Aaron Rodgers	28	22	302	4	0	151.2	104.2
Oct. 19, 2014	Aaron Rodgers	22	19	255	3	0	154.5	100.0
Nov. 9, 2014	Aaron Rodgers	27	18	315	6	0	145.8	101.2
Dec. 11, 2016	Aaron Rodgers	23	18	246	3	0	150.8	104.2
Nov. 15, 2018	Aaron Rodgers	30	21	332	2	0	128.8	108.6

Chain-Moving 100s

Boyd Dowler readies to catch a pass over Terry Brown in the Packers' 45-28 win over the St. Louis Cardinals at Lambeau Field in 1969. (Photo courtesy of the Green Bay Press-Gazette)

On any given Sunday, a player might gain 100 yards receiving.
Other times, that individual might fail to reach 100, but earn a first down with every catch he makes.

Every so often, an athlete does both.

Say hello to the chain-moving 100-yard receiver. Competitors who accumulate 100 yards receiving in a single game while bringing a first down with every pass they snag are chain-movers.

The passing game has been the Packers' forte since Curly Lambeau captained the team in the 1920s. An impressive lineup of receivers has been shagging balls in this long-running, pitch-and-catch show that is firmly embedded in Titletown.

Charlie Mathys turned in the first known 100-yard receiving performance in Packers history. The back caught eight passes for 123 yards in a 24-3 loss to the Racine Legion in 1923.

But Mathys was not a chain mover. Two of his catches did not yield first downs.

Dick Flaherty became the first chain-moving 100-yard receiver in 1926. He caught four passes for 112 yards and four first downs in the Packers' 35-0 drubbing of the Racine Tornadoes.

Green Bay has been home to 388 100-yard receiving performances. The team's record when one or more players hits or exceeds 100 yards is 227-127-7 (.639).

Green Bay has given rise to exactly 100 chain-moving episodes. The team's record when one or more players rises to this level is 69-28-2 (.707).

Only once have two players been chain-movers in the same game. Carroll Dale and Boyd Dowler teamed up to do so in closing out the 1960s.

The Packers' game with the St. Louis Cardinals on December 21, 1969, wasn't particularly important. It didn't carry with it any playoff implications. It was not going to crown either team a division champion.

No, the trappings surrounding this game were far more modest. Green Bay (7-6), which had won five NFL titles during the decade, could finish on a high note. St. Louis (4-8-1) had far less to play for, having already ensured itself of its 21st consecutive season without a postseason appearance.

Dowler and Dale were the oldest two receivers on the field. Dowler had been drafted in the third round by Green Bay in 1959. Dale, a rookie in 1960, had arrived by means of a trade with the Los Angeles Rams in 1965.

Dowler had led the Packers in receiving five times (1963-65, 1967-68). Dale was about to supplant Dowler in this capacity in 1969.

Throwing to this experienced duo, as well as to others, was Don Horn. Horn was a third-year pro, drafted in the first round by Green Bay in 1967.

Horn was a relative newcomer. The Cardinals game would be just the fifth start of his career.

The former understudy to Bart Starr had been thrust to the forefront after Starr separated his shoulder against the Detroit Lions on November 23. Including a game with the Pittsburgh Steelers on November 2, Horn was 3-1 as a starter heading into the finale with St. Louis.

The stars – Dale, Dowler and Horn – aligned against the Cardinals. Horn passed for a then-team record 410 yards and five scores. Dowler (102) and Dale (195) combined for 297 receiving yards and four touchdowns in Green Bay's 45-28 romp.

The Packers scored on five of their first six possessions. It might have been six straight had Perry Williams not lost a fumble at the Cardinals' 7-yard line late in the first quarter.

Horn's first completion went to Dowler for 16 yards. His last went to Dale for Green Bay's final touchdown.

All together, Horn completed 22 of 31 passes. He hit on 13 of his first 15 as the Packers erected a 28-14 lead.

Either Dale or Dowler had at least one reception on each of Green Bay's five touchdown drives. Dowler reached the end zone on passes of 7 and 43 yards in the first half. Dale crossed over on gains of 34 and 10 in the second half.

The duo came away with 15 first downs. In all but one case, they delivered more than the required yardage to earn a first down.

"Sunday was Funday" proclaimed Len Wagner in a *Green Bay Press-Gazette* column that ran Tuesday after the Packers' victory. The sports editor wrote: "It was probably the most purely entertaining game we've seen in a long time. There was nothing riding on it ... no tension. The players were loose. The fans were loose. There were a lot of points ... and the Packers won handily."

Dale's nine catches were a career best. His 195 receiving yards were the second-highest total posted in 1969, behind only the 197 of the Steelers' Jon Gilliam.

"I caught all four passes on (Roger) Wehrli in the first half," Dale explained. "We flopped the other way in the second half and I caught the other five on the other cornerback Nate Wright."

Wehrli and Wright were rookies. No team gave up more yards passing than the Cardinals in 1969.

Dale registered the most chain-moving, 100-yard receiving outings in Packers history with 11. He had three in both 1966 and 1969.

Flight No. 100-FD

Packers with the most chain-moving 100-yard games.

In the case of this statistic, any TD reception is also considered a first-down reception, even though the NFL did not adopt that way of thinking until 1947.

Player	No.	Player	No.
Carroll Dale	11	Paul Coffman	2
Don Hutson	9	Sterling Sharpe	2
Boyd Dowler	8	Marquez Valdes-Scantling	2
Bill Howton	7	Aundra Thompson	1
Max McGee	7	Derrick Mayes	1
James Lofton	6	Dick Flaherty	1
Bill Schroeder	5	Harry Jacunski	1
Antonio Freeman	4	Javon Walker	1
Greg Jennings	4	Jermichael Finley	1
James Jones	3	John Jefferson	1
Robert Brooks	3	Ken Payne	1
Walter Stanley	3	Ollie Smith	1
Clyde Goodnight	2	Paul Hornung	1
Corey Bradford	2	Perry Kemp	1
Donald Driver	2	Phillip Epps	1
Jordy Nelson	2	Steve Odom	1
Mark Chmura	2	Terry Glenn	1

The Power Ball is 10

Against the Detroit Lions in 1960, Tom Moore was part of an 11-play touchdown drive that consisted entirely of running plays. (Photo courtesy of the Green Bay Press-Gazette)

Fuzzy Thurston sat with his feet in a bucket of ice water. Nearby, Jerry Kramer applied heat to his knee.

The two Packers guards were nursing injuries received during a particularly physical encounter with the Detroit Lions. Kramer, in fact, had to be helped from the field in the third quarter.

On October 2, 1960, the Green and Gold stayed primarily on the ground in defeating their old rivals 28-9. Snap after brutal snap, Thurston and Kramer crashed into their counterparts across the line as they opened holes for Jim Taylor, Paul Hornung, Tom Moore and others.

Their efforts and those of their teammates paid off. Green Bay rushed for 255 yards on 52 carries and three touchdowns.

Taylor was the leader of the pack, gaining 151 yards on 26 carries.

"I didn't have any idea how much I was gaining," the fullback said. "You know, you get hit, you get up, you're groggy. You know you gained something, that's all. But you don't know how much."

Hornung was second with 73 yards on 14 tries. Moore (6 for 14) came in when Hornung needed a breather.

"Moore is a good replacement for Hornung," Packers coach Vince Lombardi explained. "Not only did Moore run well, but Hornung went back like a tiger after a rest."

Green Bay accomplished a feat against the Lions that harkened back to the early days of professional football. The Packers played power ball, orchestrating a touchdown drive that consisted of 11 plays, all runs by Taylor, Hornung and Moore.

Rare indeed is the touchdown drive of 10 or more plays that does not involve at least one pass attempt. It is a practice that has fallen out of favor, much like punting on third down.

The Packers have launched 15 power drives during the regular season dating to 1921. Eight were birthed during the 1920s. Three players carried the load on most of those excursions. Usually, the back to first lug the ball was not the one to score.

A handful of players powered up more often than most. Verne Lewellen carried on six different power drives, while Curly Lambeau did so on five. Myrt Basing and Rex Enright were three-time participants.

Basing, with three touchdowns, is the only Packer to account for more than one score. He reached the end zone on each of the three drives he initiated.

Green Bay staged its first power drive on September 30, 1923. Basing, Lambeau and Stan Mills combined for 10 rushes and 40 yards in a 12-0 win over the Minneapolis Marines.

On November 14, 1926, Enright, Lambeau and Lewellen figured in the drive involving the most plays. Fourteen times the three set sail as the Packers traveled 50 yards to pay dirt. Lewellen cashed in on a 5-yard run in Green Bay's 14-0 conquest of the Louisville Colonels.

Because at least 10 plays are involved, most of these journeys don't feature big gains. Dorsey Levens' 30-yard dash in 1997 is the longest.

The Packers' overland assault against the Lions in 1960 was not planned. Lombardi originally thought his team could pass its way to victory.

That changed after Lamar McHan was intercepted by linebacker Max Messner in the second quarter. The next time Green Bay gained possession, it stayed grounded.

Starting at the Detroit 49, Hornung carried three times for 15 yards. Taylor chipped in nine on two tries, including four on third-and-one.

Moore then replaced Hornung. He gained a yard, Taylor got seven, and Moore picked up another stripe.

That set up fourth-and-one from the Lions' 16. Taylor churned to a fresh set of downs with a four-yard thrust, and Moore finished the advance with two pokes – the last a 5-yard jaunt into the end zone.

The three earthmovers had carried the Packers to a 7-6 lead. The ground assault only intensified as Green Bay staked claim to well over half its rushing output in the third and fourth quarters.

"Our tackling was poor," admitted Lions coach George Wilson. "It wasn't just our linebackers who missed tackles, it was everybody."

Detroit sorely missed Joe Schmidt, its top-flight middle linebacker who sat out the contest with a dislocated shoulder.

So overpowering were the Packers they nearly requisitioned another power drive in the third quarter. The team moved 68 yards in 11 plays to set up Taylor's 2-yard touchdown run. Everything occurred on the ground – except for a 9-yard pass from McHan to receiver Max McGee on the third play of the advance.

Green Bay's most recent power drive occurred on November 23, 1997, in a 45-17 rout of the Dallas Cowboys at Lambeau Field. The 11-play, 88-yard, fourth-quarter movement shed four minutes, seven seconds from the clock.

Of the 15 power drives the Packers have produced, that is the only one for which a time of possession can be determined. The others occurred before official scorers thought to jot down how much time remained when the ball changed hands.

Nevertheless, it is likely the Packers' other 14 demonstrations of brute force were long-running, demoralizing affairs for the opposition as well. Green Bay lost only once – to the Chicago Cardinals on opening day 1937 – in a game in which it played power ball.

Run to Pay Dirt

Touchdown drives of 10 or more plays in which not a single pass was attempted.

Date	No-Yds	First Carry	Last Carry	Others
Sept. 30, 1923	10-40	Myrt Basing	Myrt Basing	Curly Lambeau, Stan Mills
Nov. 11, 1923	10-43	Stan Mills	Stan Mills	Lambeau, Buck Gavin
Nov. 16, 1924	10-44	Curly Lambeau	Dutch Hendrian	Verne Lewellen
Sept. 20, 1925	10-30	Myrt Basing	Myrt Basing	Jack Harris, Lewellen
Nov. 1, 1925	13-59	Myrt Basing	Myrt Basing	Charlie Mathys, Lambeau, Marty Norton
Oct. 24, 1926	12-52	Rex Enright	Jack Harris	Eddie Kotal, Pid Purdy, Lewellen
Nov. 14, 1926	14-50	Rex Enright	Verne Lewellen	Lambeau
Sept. 18, 1927	12-46	Rex Enright	Curly Lambeau	Lewellen
Nov. 2, 1930	11-51	Bo Molenda	Paul Fitzgibbon	Herdis McCrary, Arnie Herber, Lewellen
Nov. 26, 1931	10-50	Bo Molenda	Bo Molenda	Faye Wilson
Oct. 30, 1932	10-43	Herdis McCrary	Hank Bruder	Weert Engelmann
Sept. 12, 1937	10-66	Paul Miller	Clarke Hinkle	Joe Laws, Don Hutson, Herm Schneidman
Dec. 1, 1946	10-66	Walt Schlinkman	Ted Fritsch	Tony Canadeo, Bob Forte
Oct. 2, 1960	11-49	Paul Hornung	Tom Moore	Jim Taylor
Nov. 23, 1997	11-88	Dorsey Levens	Dorsey Levens	William Henderson, Brett Favre

The Whole Enchilada

Ted Fritsch (far right) rips off some yardage against the Chicago Bears at City Stadium. (Photo courtesy of the Green Bay Press-Gazette)

Football, it has been said, is the ultimate team sport.
 As with any group effort, however, contributions from individual members aren't always equal. One player can rise above the rest.

On December 1, 1946, Ted Fritsch staged a one-man show unmatched in Packers history. The fullback scored every point in Green Bay's 20-7 victory over the Washington Redskins.

Not bad for a veteran who, four years earlier, had doubts he'd make the squad.

The Packers have played 116 regular-season games since 1921 in which only one player scored all the team's points. In all but 11 cases, that lone individual tallied fewer than 10 points.

Relying on one scorer has not been conducive to winning. Green Bay's record is a miserable 26-83-7 (.254) when a second scorer fails to emerge.

Furthermore, most of those 26 victories (15) were posted during an era (pre-1936) when points were few and far between. Since 1968, the Packers have won just five of their 52 single-scorer outings.

Green Bay dropped 23 straight such games from 1968 through 1979.

Mason Crosby delivered the most recent win. The placekicker booted field goals of 20, 41 and 40 yards to down the New York Jets 9-0 in East Rutherford, New Jersey, on Halloween 2010.

Crosby's afternoon is typical of many of these efforts. Since 1962, 49 of the team's 55 single-scorer affairs have involved field goals only.

So who are these lone wolves, these rugged individuals who were afforded no help on the scoreboard?

Forty-nine Packers have been solo artists. Chester Marcol (16), Jan Stenerud (7), Verne Lewellen (6), Don Hutson (6) and Fritsch (6) charted most often.

Curly Lambeau was the first. His field goals were all Green Bay could muster in a 13-3 loss to the Rock Island Independents on October 30, 1921, and in a 3-3 tie with the Chicago Cardinals three weeks later.

Fritsch tallied the most points. His performance against the Washington Redskins remains the team standard. No one else has put up more than 13 points in a one-man display.

Green Bay didn't draft Fritsch. He was recommended to the team by a former Packer, Eddie Kotal.

Kotal had played five seasons (1925-29) in Green Bay. He then spent 11 years coaching at Central State Teachers College (now the University of Wisconsin-Stevens Point).

Kotal rejoined the Packers as the team's backfield coach in 1942. He suggested Green Bay take a look at Fritsch, a rugged player who had been named all-conference as a junior and senior while playing for Kotal at Stevens Point.

"I took enough clothes with me for three days," Fritsch recalled years later in an interview published in the *New Castle News* of Pennsylvania. "I never thought I'd be lucky enough to make the grade with men like (Don) Hutson, (Cecil) Isbell, (Baby) Ray and (Charley and Lou) Brock. I'd never played ball before more than 3,000 fans in my life."

That the Packers had lost three fullbacks – Clarke Hinkle, Ed Jankowski and George Paskvan – to the armed services helped Fritsch's cause. The newcomer, who was 4-F because of a punctured ear drum, not only made the team, he missed just one game in nine seasons (1942-50) in Green Bay.

As a rookie, Fritsch led the Packers in rushing (323 yards). He was the team's leading ground gainer two other times: 1944 (322) and 1945 (282).

The durable back also tried his foot at placekicking. He made 7-of-15 field goal attempts in his first four seasons and was successful on his only try for an extra point.

Fritsch became the team's primary kicker in 1946. Hutson, who had led the club in scoring seven years running, retired after the 1945 season.

Fritsch responded by leading the league in scoring. His 100 points accounted for more than two-thirds of Green Bay's outlay of 148.

Fritsch was a lone scorer four times in 1946. He tallied 13 points in losses to the Bears (10-7) and Cardinals (24-6), and he provided 29 points in victories at Detroit (9-0) and Washington (20-7).

Green Bay rushed for 301 yards against the Redskins at Griffith Stadium. Walt Schlinkman (17-96), Tony Canadeo (16-93) and Fritsch (17-59) had 50 of the team's 64 rushing attempts.

Others beside Fritsch had opportunities to score. Green Bay ran 22 plays inside Washington's red zone. In addition to Fritsch, eight other Packers were either given the ball on running plays or were targeted by quarterback Jug Girard on passing plays initiated within 20 yards of the Redskins' goal line.

Fritsch was the only one to reach the end zone.

The big fullback put Green Bay up 7-0 on a 1-yard plunge midway through the second quarter. He again scored from a yard out in the third.

He counted for a third time after Paul Lipscomb recovered a bad snap on Washington's 39-yard line. Fritsch covered that distance in two plays, racing 25 yards for a first down before cashing in on a 14-yard burst to close out the day's scoring.

Fritsch could have had even more points. He misfired on three field goal attempts, and his second extra-point attempt veered to the right.

Still, the 20 points he did post remain the most in a game in which only one player did all the scoring for the Packers.

Fritsch was a consensus all-pro in 1946. Shortly after the season ended, he signed a contract with the Oshkosh All-Stars of the National Basketball League to play guard.

The amiable fullback continued to play for the Packers through the 1950 season. He again led the team in scoring in 1947 (56), 1948 (29) and 1949 (32).

Fritsch was cut just days before the season opener in 1951. With 11 points, he had been the team's second-leading scorer during the preseason behind Jack Cloud (12).

"It wasn't easy to place Ted Fritsch on waivers," head coach Gene Ronzani said, "because he was a true Packer."

Single-Source Scoring

Games in which one player scored all of the Packers' points (minimum 10 points).

Player	Date	Points	Opponent	Result
Ted Fritsch	Dec. 1, 1946	20	Redskins	GB won 20-7
Curly Lambeau	Nov. 26, 1922	13	Badgers	GB won 13-0
Clarke Hinkle	Dec. 10, 1935	13	Eagles	GB won 13-6
Paul Hornung	Dec. 10, 1960	13	49ers	GB won 13-0
Myrt Basing	Sept. 30, 1923	12	Marines	GB won 12-0
Verne Lewellen	Sept. 30, 1928	12	Bears	GB tied 12-12
Lavvie Dilweg	Nov. 17, 1929	12	Cardinals	GB won 12-0
Chester Marcol	Sept. 7, 1980	12	Bears	GB won 12-6
Jan Stenerud	Dec. 12, 1983	12	Buccaneers	GB won 12-9
Al Del Greco	Sept. 22, 1986	12	Bears	GB lost 12-25
Paul Hornung	Nov. 24, 1960	10	Lions	GB lost 10-23

Catch of Characters

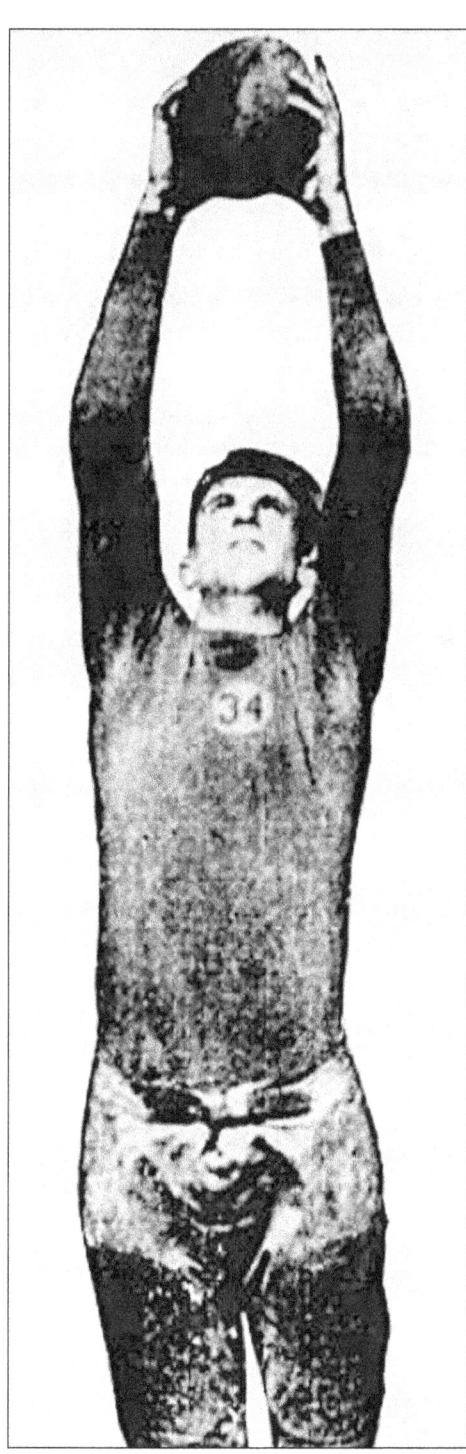

LaVern (Lavvie) Dilweg played every minute of the 1927 season. (Photo courtesy of the Green Bay Press-Gazette)

Had LaVern (Lavvie) Dilweg been asked which year of his life was most memorable, he might have chosen 1927.

In May, he graduated from Marquette University with a law degree. Law remained front and center throughout the remainder of his existence.

In June, he married Eleanor Coleman, a member of the 1924 Olympic swimming team. The couple celebrated their 40th wedding anniversary months before Dilweg's death in 1968.

In August, he signed with the Packers. He played eight years with the club (1927-34), and was a consensus all-pro during his first four seasons in Green Bay.

Despite his stellar play, Dilweg is not enshrined in the Pro Football Hall of Fame in Canton. One reason: only four players whose careers began in the 1920s have been inducted since 1967.

Long gone are the men who could attest to the greatness of those who played when town teams did business. Were his peers alive, the story might be different as Dilweg is generally regarded as the best end in the NFL's first 15 years of play.

First, he was reliable. Dilweg played in 98 of a possible 104 games during his career. The 39 games in which he participated during the team's triple championship run (1929-31) are tied for the most by any player (Herdis McCrary, Mike Michalske and Bo Molenda).

Second, he was rugged. Dilweg is the only Packer not listed as having been replaced by a substitute in any game in 1927. If the summaries published in the *Green Bay Press-Gazette* are accurate, Dilweg was a 60-minute man for the entire 10-game season, a remarkable accomplishment.

Third, Dilweg was the first Packer to catch 100 passes. Roughly two-thirds of his haul was amassed during his first four seasons in Green Bay.

Finally, as a defender, Dilweg's quickness, anticipation, and long arms proved too much for many an opponent. He could rush the passer, cover receivers or stop a running back in his tracks.

"I always enjoyed defense," Dilweg told Terry Bledsoe of *The Milwaukee Journal* in 1965. "Nowadays, of course, the game is full of specialists and they're wonderful at their jobs. But for me, if I had not been permitted to play both offense and defense, I'm sure I wouldn't have enjoyed it as much as I did."

Offensively, Dilweg holds a Packers record that has never been recognized. He caught passes from the greatest number of players in team history.

Versatility was far more important in the 1920s than today. Roster sizes were small, and those on the team had to contribute in a variety of ways.

During each season – indeed, during each game – receivers could expect to catch passes from more than one teammate. At least two – and sometimes as many as six – launched throws in every game from 1927 through 1930.

Red Dunn was the first to connect with Dilweg. The duo had played together at Marquette University for two seasons (1922-23).

Throughout the remainder of 1927, Dilweg also caught passes from Curly Lambeau, Marty Bross and Eddie Kotal. In the seasons that followed, he accepted throws from Johnny Blood, Hank Bruder, Paul Fitzgibbon, Arnie Herber, Clarke Hinkle, Verne Lewellen, Larry Marks, Herdis McCrary, Bo Molenda, Bob Monnett and Russ Saunders.

In all, Dilweg caught passes from at least 15 different individuals. That number could be higher, as play-by-plays are not available for some of the games in which he toiled.

Of course, most players who persist long enough wind up fielding passes from more than one source. Only two players in Packers history have caught more than 50 with each having come from the same quarterback: Derrick Mayes (54 from Brett Favre) and Keith Jackson (53 from Favre).

But while relying on multiple passers is all but inevitable, working with more than eight is uncommon. Just 16 receivers can make that claim.

Dilweg, of course, is at the top having collaborated with at least 15 different passers. Tony Canadeo tied Dilweg in October 1952 after he snagged one from rookie quarterback Babe Parilli.

Others high on the list are Don Hutson (13), John Brockington (13) and Rich McGeorge (13). Blood (12) and Lewellen (12) finished with a dozen partners.

Dilweg established his record for diversity in the third quarter of the 1933 season finale. He safeguarded an 11-yard pitch from Monnett (teammate No. 15) near midfield in a 7-6 loss to the Chicago Bears at Wrigley Field.

A year later, Dilweg caught just five passes total. He announced his retirement on August 31, 1935.

"I had a couple of more years left, I think, but I could feel myself slowing down," Dilweg said in 1965. "Bruises that had healed in a week were taking 10 days. And they didn't want to pay me what I thought I ought to get, so I thought I would just get out of it."

Dilweg began practicing law during his playing days. He was elected to Congress in 1942. President John Kennedy appointed him to the U.S. Foreign Claims Commission in 1961.

In December 1927, Wilfred Smith of the *Chicago Tribune* named Dilweg as one of two ends on his All American Pro Team. The honor capped an unforgettable year that had to rank high in Dilweg's event-filled life.

Eight is Not Enough

Receivers who caught passes from more than eight different passers during their Packers careers, and the one with whom they collaborated most often.

Player	No.	Most Frequent
Lavvie Dilweg	15	Arnie Herber
Tony Canadeo	15	Tobin Rote
Don Hutson	13	Cecil Isbell
Rich McGeorge	13	John Hadl
John Brockington	13	John Hadl
Johnny Blood	12	Arnie Herber
Verne Lewellen	11	Curly Lambeau
Milt Gantenbein	11	Arnie Herber
Nolan Luhn	11	Jack Jacobs
Max McGee	11	Bart Starr
Ed West	11	Don Majkowski
Eddie Kotal	10	Verne Lewellen
Carroll Dale	10	Bart Starr
Joe Laws	9	Bob Monnett
Steve Odom	9	Lynn Dickey
James Lofton	9	Lynn Dickey

Fourmen

Packers players who scored three or more touchdowns on fourth down.

Player	Rushing TDs	Receiving TDs	Total TDs
Verne Lewellen	9	4	13
Jim Taylor	10	1	11
Don Hutson	0	8	8
Clarke Hinkle	5	0	5
Gerry Ellis	4	0	4
Barty Smith	3	0	3
James Lofton	0	3	3
Johnny Blood	0	3	3
Randall Cobb	0	3	3
Rex Enright	1	2	3
Ted Fritsch	3	0	3
Tobin Rote	3	0	3

Fore!

The Packers' longest scoring plays on fourth down with date, distance to go, and play details.

Date	Dist	Play	Opponent
Nov. 19, 1972	2	Dave Davis 68 pass from Ron Widby	Oilers
Dec. 29, 2013	8	Randall Cobb 48 pass from Aaron Rodgers	Bears
Nov. 10, 2003	1	Ahman Green 45 run	Eagles
Sept. 28, 1941	5	Don Hutson 45 pass from Cecil Isbell	Bears
Nov. 26, 1950	10	Breezy Reid 44 pass from Paul Christman	49ers
Sept. 18, 1966	1	Paul Hornung 44 pass from Bart Starr	Browns
Nov. 29, 2004	1	Najeh Davenport 40 run	Rams
Nov. 2, 1924	5	Tillie Voss 40 pass from Curly Lambeau	Racine Legion
Sept. 25, 2005	4	Robert Ferguson 37 pass from Brett Favre	Buccaneers
Sept. 15, 2013	3	Randall Cobb 35 pass from Aaron Rodgers	Redskins

Fourth-and-Six

Tight end Tom Crabtree hustles downfield with a fourth-down pass on a fake field goal against the Chicago Bears in 2012. (Photo courtesy of the Green Bay Press-Gazette)

Fourth-and-26 conjures up painful memories for Packers fans of a certain age. Twenty-six yards on that down was the distance the Philadelphia Eagles overcame to beat Green Bay 20-17 in a divisional playoff game in January 2004.

But there is another fourth-and-26 in team lore. It involved a punter, a backup tight end, and how the two conspired to help send a longtime rival to defeat.

Going for it on fourth down can take moxie. Sometimes it requires nothing more than desperation. Failure to secure the necessary yardage, of course, can be deflating. There is no fifth down in football.

The Packers have gone for it on fourth down more than 1,400 times since 1923. They have done so every year, from a high of 41 times (at least) in 1951 to a low of five in both 1961 and 1997.

More often than not, Green Bay has scored at least one touchdown on a fourth-down play in a season. The team set a record with seven in 1926. Six players reached the end zone on fourth down that year. Verne Lewellen was the only player to do so twice.

No Packers player scored more fourth-down touchdowns than Lewellen. The halfback cantered into the end zone 13 times in nine seasons (1924-32) on that final down, two better than runner-up Jim Taylor.

Lewellen was a gifted runner, skilled pass receiver and occasional passer. By all accounts, he was the most effective punter of his day during a time when field position was all important.

The News Record of Neenah, Wisconsin, ran a short piece after Lewellen signed his rookie contract following his college career at Nebraska. In part, the story read: "In the game against Notre Dame, Lewellen punts averaged 60 yards. One of his kicks, early in the contest, traveled 69 yards. Throughout the season, his trusty booting got the Cornhuskers out of many a tight hole."

David Beverly has long been recognized as the player who punted most often (495 times) for Green Bay. In reality, Lewellen holds that honor, as he sent the pigskin down the field more than 600 times.

Games stories from his era are replete with mentions of how he outkicked the competition. He was a master at pinning opponents inside the 20.

Lewellen also had a nose for the end zone. He tallied more points than any other Packers player during the team's first 12 years.

Lewellen scored 51 touchdowns and one point-after for a total of 307 points. Johnny Blood was next with 162, just over half of Lewellen's total.

For five straight years (1926-30), Lewellen was Green Bay's leading scorer.

The rookie found pay dirt for the first time on fourth down against the Milwaukee Badgers on November 16, 1924. His one-yard plunge put the Packers up by 10 en route to a 17-10 victory.

A year later, he ventured across the goal line with a fourth-down pass for the first time. Charlie Mathys found him from two yards out in Green Bay's 14-10 conquest of the Chicago Bears.

Lewellen became the third and final member of a select group in 1929. In tossing a 3-yard touchdown pass to Herdis McCrary against the Giants in New York, he joined Curly Lambeau and Eddie Kotal as the only Packers to have produced a fourth-down touchdown by rushing, receiving and passing.

Lewellen's talent on fourth down translated into wins. The Packers were undefeated (12-0-1) when he was a party to a fourth-down TD.

For all the fourth-down touchdowns the team has manufactured, only once has the Green and Gold produced three in one game. It happened on October 20, 1963, in a game against the St. Louis Cardinals in which Bart Starr suffered a hairline fracture in his passing hand.

Green Bay (4-1) needed to defeat St. Louis (4-1) in order to remain within striking distance of the Bears (5-0). The Packers, who were pursuing a third straight championship, had stumbled against Chicago (10-3) in the opener.

At Busch Stadium, the Packers ran up against fourth down 10 times. Twice they punted, and four times Jerry Kramer attempted field goals (he made three).

That left four occasions when the team went for it. Tom Moore (once) and Jim Taylor (twice) came through with 1-yard TD plunges. Moore also converted in the second quarter with a 2-yard run that kept alive an advance capped six plays later by Taylor. Refusing to settle for field goals carried Green Bay to a 30-7 win.

At the time, no one commented on the novelty of having scored touchdowns on three fourth-down plays. Likely, few would have cared.

For Green Bay, Starr's health was paramount. After scrambling for 15 yards late in the third quarter, he was knocked out of bounds by Jimmy Hill.

Hill slugged Starr after claiming the quarterback had kicked him as the two tumbled out of the field of play. Hill was penalized for unsportsmanlike conduct.

Starr was momentarily knocked out. He was finished for the afternoon, and he did not attempt a pass in any of the Packers' next four games.

Meanwhile, the San Francisco 49ers aided Green Bay's cause by upsetting the Bears 20-14. With eight games remaining, Green Bay (5-1) and Chicago (5-1) were tied for first place in the Western Conference.

In November, the Bears crushed the Packers 26-7. John Roach, not Starr, quarterbacked the Green and Gold.

At season's end, Chicago (11-1-2) edged Green Bay (11-2-1) to end the Packers' dream of a third straight title. A week later, the Bears slipped past the Giants 14-7 to claim their first NFL championship since 1946.

Nearly a half century later, these bitter rivals were on the field when Green Bay again rolled the dice. The play not only generated more than enough yardage, it resulted in a touchdown.

The Packers hosted the Bears at Lambeau Field on September 13, 2012. The game was a defensive affair for much of the first half.

With just under two minutes remaining in the second quarter, the Packers lined up for an apparent field goal attempt. Mason Crosby, who had booted a 48-yarder earlier in the period for the game's only score, appeared ready to try another, this one from 45 yards away.

It's unlikely the Bears caught a whiff of Green Bay's impending chicanery. After all, the Packers needed 26 yards – all the way to the Chicago 1-yard line – to earn a first down.

At the snap, Crosby ran to his left. Holder Tim Masthay tossed a shovel pass to Tom Crabtree who was headed in the opposite direction.

Blocks by Brian Bulaga (on Eric Weems) and Evan Dietrich-Smith (on Chris Conte) opened a large hole for the backup tight end, who ran untouched into the end zone. Crabtree celebrated with a Lambeau Leap.

"Fourth-and-26 was not the plan," said Packers coach Mike McCarthy of the call. "I called that for a different reason. We've been working on that for two or three seasons. We were looking for a certain look, and the Bears gave it.

"I was trying to send the team a message. I would have been fine with the field position (if the fake had failed)."

The distance – 26 yards – was the longest ever overcome by the team on a fourth-down play that reached the end zone.

Masthay-to-Crabtree put the Packers up 10-0. Buoyed by its stubborn defense, Green Bay persevered 27-10.

"I had to double-check with Coach, 'You're really calling it right now? Are you sure?'" Crabtree said. "I knew once we called it and once we got out there and got a peek at the defense, it was going to work."

Masthay became the first Packers punter to throw a touchdown pass since Ron Widby in 1972. Widby wiped out a fourth-and-two with a 68-yard toss to Dave Davis in a 23-10 win against the Oilers in Houston. That remains the longest gain by the Packers on any fourth down.

"My hats off to Coach for making the call, because I was really surprised when he called the play because it's fourth-and-26. You know this, right?" Masthay said. "Great call."

No argument there. Except, perhaps, from the Chicago Bears.

Lists

Chris Jacke watches as one of his 224 field goal attempts heads for the uprights. Jacke is one of three Packers to have attempted more than 200 field goals while with the team. (Photo courtesy of the Green Bay Press-Gazette)

All-time 1932-2018 Rushing

Andy Uram (far left) skirts right end behind Clarke Hinkle (30) for a gain against the Cleveland Rams in the 1941 season opener. (Photo courtesy of the Green Bay Press-Gazette)

	Att.	Yds.	Avg.	LG	TD		Att.	Yds.	Avg.	LG	TD
Ahman Green	1851	8322	4.50	98	54	Floyd Reid	459	1964	4.28	69	13
Jim Taylor	1811	8207	4.53	84	81	BE Smith	544	1942	3.57	33	18
John Brockington	1293	5024	3.89	53	29	Joe Laws	470	1932	4.11		9
Tony Canadeo	1025	4197	4.09	54	26	Brett Favre	555	1786	3.22	40	13
Ryan Grant	955	4143	4.34	66	27	MacArthur Lane	484	1711	3.54	41	7
Dorsey Levens	1006	3937	3.91	52	28	Brent Fullwood	433	1702	3.93	38	18
Clarke Hinkle	1171	3860	3.30	57	34	Elijah Pitts	479	1684	3.52	34	28
Gerry Ellis	836	3826	4.58	71	25	Darrell Thompson	464	1642	3.54	60	7
Paul Hornung	893	3711	4.16	72	50	Jessie Clark	379	1588	4.19	80	9
Eddie Lacy	788	3435	4.36	60	23	Jim Grabowski	424	1582	3.73	36	8
Edgar Bennett	936	3353	3.58	39	19	Cecil Isbell	422	1522	3.61		10
Donny Anderson	787	3165	4.02	54	24	Bob Monnett	510	1488	2.92		7
Aaron Rodgers	568	2939	5.17	35	27	Walt Schlinkman	365	1455	3.99	44	8
Eddie Lee Ivery	667	2933	4.40	49	23	Brandon Jackson	347	1329	3.83	71	7
James Starks	618	2506	4.06	65	9	Bart Starr	247	1308	5.30	39	15
Tobin Rote	419	2205	5.26	55	29	Eric Torkelson	351	1307	3.72	29	8
Ted Fritsch	619	2200	3.55	55	31	Aaron Jones	214	1176	5.50	67	12
Howie Ferguson	544	2120	3.90	57	6	Fred Cone	347	1156	3.33	41	12
Tom Moore	503	2069	4.11	77	20	Andy Uram	239	1073	4.49	97	4
Terdell Middleton	559	2044	3.66	76	15	Najeh Davenport	217	1068	4.92	76	7

	Att.	Yds.	Avg.	LG	TD		Att.	Yds.	Avg.	LG	TD
Travis Williams	271	1063	3.92	39	6	Chester Johnson	101	309	3.06		1
Kenneth Davis	262	1053	4.02	50	4	Roy McKay	100	288	2.88	41	3
Don Majkowski	199	1037	5.21	33	9	Roger Grove	70	287	4.10		1
Jamaal Williams	274	1020	3.72	25	7	Don Hutson	62	284	4.58	27	3
Ed Jankowski	275	1002	3.64		8	Earl Girard	76	283	3.72	35	1
Keith Woodside	259	976	3.77	68	6	Hal Van Every	63	281	4.46		2
Willard Harrell	311	934	3.00	56	5	Noah Herron	82	271	3.30	19	3
Vince Workman	242	927	3.83	44	10	DeMond Parker	54	269	4.98	26	2
Tony Fisher	235	880	3.74	28	4	Del Rodgers	71	269	3.79	15	1
Don McIlhenny	221	854	3.86	46	3	Brett Hundley	39	268	6.87	24	2
Ty Montgomery	177	849	4.80	61	7	Chuck Sample	59	257	4.36	31	4
Lou Brock	254	804	3.17		10	Kevin Willhite	53	251	4.74	61	0
Dave Hampton	195	787	4.04	53	7	Cedric Benson	71	248	3.49	11	1
Harlan Huckleby	242	779	3.22	23	10	James Lofton	31	245	7.90	83	1
Al Carmichael	166	712	4.29	41	2	Mike Meade	69	243	3.52	19	1
Billy Grimes	145	662	4.57	73	6	David Whitehurst	77	242	3.14	19	7
George Sauer	190	656	3.45		6	Bobby Jack Floyd	61	236	3.87	17	1
Paul Ott Carruth	194	614	3.16	42	5	Raymont Harris	79	228	2.89	14	1
John Kuhn	196	601	3.07	18	15	DuJuan Harris	50	221	4.42	21	2
Reggie Cobb	153	579	3.78	30	3	Donald Driver	34	217	6.38	45	1
Samkon Gado	145	575	3.97	64	6	Jim Gillette	50	207	4.14	26	0
Hank Bruder	190	569	2.99		5	Steve Odom	16	205	12.81	28	1
Paul Miller	143	537	3.76		1	Tony Falkenstein	58	198	3.41	59	1
Vernand Morency	120	529	4.41	39	2	Larry Mason	48	194	4.04	17	0
Bruce Smith	96	522	5.44	37	1	Ralph Earhart	50	194	3.88	72	1
Irv Comp	255	502	1.97	34	7	Les Goodman	38	189	4.97	47	1
Nate Simpson	153	497	3.25	40	1	Paul Duhart	51	183	3.59	16	2
Gary Ellerson	122	492	4.03	37	5	John Stephens	48	173	3.60	22	1
Alex Green	138	475	3.44	41	0	Randy Wright	55	173	3.15	27	3
Steve Atkins	120	467	3.89	60	2	Ray Crouse	53	169	3.19	14	0
Ben Wilson	103	453	4.40	40	2	Aaron Ripkowski	39	163	4.18	15	2
Michael Haddix	142	446	3.14	13	0	Harry Sydney	51	163	3.20	19	2
Travis Jervey	109	431	3.95	16	1	Cliff Aberson	48	161	3.35	13	0
William Henderson	123	426	3.46	17	5	Veryl Switzer	31	160	5.16	38	0
Don Perkins	94	399	4.24	49	1	Joe Francis	26	158	6.08	21	1
Darick Holmes	93	386	4.15	13	1	Jim Culbreath	47	153	3.26	18	0
Joe Johnson	93	376	4.04	21	0	Aaron Hayden	32	148	4.63	21	1
Babe Parilli	106	375	3.54	20	7	Frank Balazs	38	147	3.87		1
Charles Goldenberg	107	365	3.41		6	Herman Fontenot	34	145	4.26	19	1
Lew Carpenter	64	359	5.61	55	1	Terry Wells	33	139	4.21	25	0
Earl Gros	77	358	4.65	26	4	Jack Jacobs	42	137	3.26	23	2
Randall Cobb	59	352	5.97	67	0	Ricky Patton	37	134	3.62	14	0
Johnny Blood	96	351	3.66		0	Lamar McHan	24	131	5.46	35	1
DeShawn Wynn	64	332	5.19	73	5	Basil Mitchell	31	125	4.03	15	0
Bob Forte	107	331	3.09	25	0	Phillip Epps	10	121	12.10	34	1
Perry Williams	103	329	3.19	14	1	Max McGee	12	121	10.08	36	0
Larry Coutre	63	322	5.11	53	1	Bill Reichardt	39	121	3.10	14	1
Ed Cody	82	321	3.91	51	2	Larry Buhler	41	121	2.95		0

	Att.	Yds.	Avg.	LG	TD		Att.	Yds.	Avg.	LG	TD
Jerry Tagge	41	117	2.85	41	3	DeShone Kizer	5	39	7.80	12	0
George Paskvan	38	116	3.05	12	0	Dave Kopay	10	39	3.90	20	0
Anthony Dilweg	21	114	5.43	22	0	Jeff Janis	2	38	19.00	19	1
Christine Michael	31	114	3.68	42	1	John Jefferson	4	38	9.50	15	0
Jack Cloud	47	113	2.40	19	4	James Hargrove	11	38	3.45	7	1
Johnathan Franklin	19	107	5.63	51	1	Herm Schneidman	13	37	2.85		0
Jim Jensen	36	107	2.97	15	0	Zeke Bratkowski	25	35	1.40	13	1
Chuck Mercein	31	105	3.39	15	2	Dick Weisgerber	11	34	3.09		0
Bob Summerhays	29	101	3.48	14	0	Freddie Parker	8	33	4.13	17	0
Allen Rice	30	100	3.33	21	0	Don Jackson	10	32	3.20	7	0
OE Smith	36	100	2.78	11	0	John Roach	6	31	5.17	22	1
Lynn Dickey	129	98	0.76	13	9	Jim Shanley	23	30	1.30	5	0
LeShon Johnson	28	97	3.46	43	0	Marquez Valdes-Scantling	2	29	14.50	21	0
Dimitri Nance	36	95	2.64	11	0	Herb Banet	9	29	3.22		0
Mike Tomczak	17	93	5.47	48	1	Byron Bailey	13	29	2.23	13	0
Fred Provo	29	90	3.10	28	0	Boyd Dowler	2	28	14.00	20	0
Scott Hunter	51	90	1.76	16	10	Ken Roskie	5	28	5.60	9	1
Walt Landers	24	81	3.38	14	0	Bobby Douglass	4	27	6.75	17	0
Wuert Engelmann	23	79	3.43		0	Nick Luchey	11	27	2.45	4	0
Robert Brooks	17	75	4.41	21	0	Raven Greene	1	26	26.00	26	0
Rondell Mealey	22	73	3.32	18	1	Lee Weigel	10	26	2.60	7	0
Sterling Sharpe	23	72	3.13	26	0	Randy Johnson	5	25	5.00	11	1
Antonio Chatman	12	70	5.83	18	0	Jon Staggers	5	25	5.00	20	1
Matt Flynn	58	70	1.21	17	1	Clyde Goodnight	9	25	2.78	12	0
Brandon Saine	18	69	3.83	10	0	Stan Heath	10	25	2.50	18	1
Alan Risher	11	64	5.82	15	1	Jerry Norton	3	24	8.00	24	0
Bob Hudson	15	62	4.13	17	0	JR Boone	7	24	3.43	24	0
Don Chandler	2	60	30.00	33	0	Dom Moselle	12	23	1.92	7	1
Walter Stanley	6	58	9.67	24	0	Frank Purnell	5	22	4.40	7	0
Blair Kiel	9	55	6.11	20	1	Larry Hickman	7	22	3.14	4	0
Scott Tolzien	8	52	6.50	19	1	Earl Witte	8	22	2.75		0
Bob Cifers	23	52	2.26	19	0	John Crockett	9	21	2.33	12	0
Arnie Herber	173	52	0.30		1	Clarence Self	0	21		21	0
Bill Butler	7	49	7.00	16	0	Bill Howton	4	20	5.00	11	0
Carlos Brown	12	49	4.08	21	0	John Sterling	5	20	4.00	9	0
Russ Mosely	16	49	3.06	9	0	Kregg Lumpkin	1	19	19.00	19	0
Ben Starret	16	48	3.00	13	2	Charles Casper	4	19	4.75		0
Cliff Taylor	14	47	3.36	17	1	Beattie Feathers	4	19	4.75		0
Ray Pelfrey	3	44	14.67	24	0	Alonzo Harris	4	19	4.75	16	0
Johnny Papit	6	44	7.33	21	1	Lavale Thomas	5	19	3.80	5	0
John Hadl	28	44	1.57	9	0	Buford McGee	8	19	2.38	4	0
Jack Losch	19	43	2.26	8	0	Randy Walker	1	18	18.00	18	0
Bob Nussbaumer	29	43	1.48	16	0	Carroll Dale	3	18	6.00	9	0
Perry Kemp	6	42	7.00	14	0	Gib Dawson	5	18	3.60	18	0
Walter Williams	6	42	7.00	28	0	Paul Christman	7	18	2.57	4	1
Don Milan	4	41	10.25	15	0	Larry Morris	8	18	2.25	10	0
Don Barton	7	40	5.71	14	0	David Beverly	9	18	2.00	11	0
Jeff Query	3	39	13.00	18	0	Bill Schroeder	3	17	5.67	12	0

	Att.	Yds.	Avg.	LG	TD		Att.	Yds.	Avg.	LG	TD
Antonio Freeman	8	17	2.13	14	0	Charles Jordan	1	5	5.00	5	0
Allen Rossum	1	16	16.00	16	0	Koren Robinson	1	5	5.00	5	0
Steve Wagner	1	16	16.00	16	0	Barry Smith	1	5	5.00	5	0
Gary Lewis	4	16	4.00	11	1	Gerald Tinker	1	5	5.00	5	0
Dave Osborn	6	16	2.67	6	0	Wayland Becker	2	5	2.50	3	0
Bill Boedecker	8	16	2.00	8	0	Frank Patrick	2	5	2.50	3	0
Larry Craig	10	16	1.60	4	0	Allen Jacobs	3	5	1.67	2	0
Reshard Lee	11	16	1.45	4	0	VR Anderson	4	5	1.25	4	0
Claudis James	1	15	15.00	15	0	Knile Davis	5	5	1.00	4	0
Larry Krause	6	15	2.50	12	0	Frank Mestnick	1	4	4.00	4	0
Ken Keuper	6	14	2.33	8	0	Bill Robinson	3	4	1.33	4	0
Aundra Thompson	12	14	1.17	16	0	Rip Collins	5	4	0.80	6	0
Trevor Davis	2	13	6.50	9	0	Paul Coffman	1	3	3.00	3	0
Leland Glass	2	13	6.50	13	0	Jay Graham	1	3	3.00	3	0
Tim Masthay	2	13	6.50	7	0	Rich McGeorge	1	3	3.00	3	0
Buster Mott	5	13	2.60		0	Don Zimmerman	1	3	3.00	3	0
Jim Ringo	0	13		13	0	Kelly Cook	2	3	1.50	2	0
Junior Coffey	3	12	4.00	10	0	Michael Blair	2	3	1.50	2	0
Javon Walker	3	12	4.00	11	0	Aubrey Matthews	3	3	1.00	4	0
Richard Rodgers	1	11	11.00	11	0	Charles Wilson	3	3	1.00	5	0
Ed Frutig	1	11	11.00	11	0	Marcus Wilson	6	3	0.50	5	0
Paul Staroba	1	11	11.00	11	0	Jim Salsbury	0	3		3	0
Dexter McNabb	2	11	5.50	8	0	Kapri Bibbs	1	2	2.00	2	0
Chuck Fusina	7	11	1.57	6	0	Al Cannava	1	2	2.00	2	0
Craig Nall	10	11	1.10	9	0	Harry Mattos	1	2	2.00	2	0
Corey Harris	2	10	5.00	7	0	Claude Perry	1	2	2.00	2	0
Ken Snelling	3	10	3.33	8	0	Patrick Scott	1	2	2.00	2	0
Hurdis McCrary	6	10	1.67		0	Alex Urban	1	2	2.00	2	0
Matt Hasselbeck	10	10	1.00	13	0	Rich Campbell	2	2	1.00	5	0
Bob Mann	2	9	4.50	9	0	Patrick Collins	2	2	1.00	2	0
Ron Kramer	6	9	1.50	12	0	Jim Lankas	2	2	1.00	1	0
Clarence Thompson	6	9	1.50		0	Lee Morris	2	2	1.00	4	0
Bob Kahler	9	9	1.00	13	0	Lindell Pearson	2	2	1.00	2	0
Jim Zorn	10	9	0.90	8	0	Ed West	2	2	1.00	2	1
Paul Held	1	8	8.00	8	0	Perry Moss	5	2	0.40	2	0
Jermaine Whitehead	1	7	7.00	7	0	Jackie Harris	1	1	1.00	1	0
Ward Cuff	1	7	7.00	7	0	Dale Livingston	1	1	1.00	1	0
Eric Metcalf	2	7	3.50	5	0	BJ Raji	1	1	1.00	1	1
Jack Concannon	3	7	2.33	6	1	Devante Mays	4	1	0.25	2	0
Mark Brunell	6	7	1.17	5	1	Jim DelGaizo	4	1	0.25	3	0
Don Highsmith	7	7	1.00	4	0	Ty Detmer	4	1	0.25	5	0
John Howell	7	7	1.00		0	Herman Rohrig	42	1	0.02	18	0
MD Jennings	1	6	6.00	6	0	Wally Dreyer	1	0	0.00	0	0
TJ Rubley	2	6	3.00	6	0	Vince Ferragamo	1	0	0.00	0	0
John Kirby	3	6	2.00	8	0	Derrick Frost	1	0	0.00	0	0
Equanimeous St. Brown	1	5	5.00	5	0	Tony Hunter	1	0	0.00	0	0
Bob Adkins	1	5	5.00	5	0	Joe Kerridge	1	0	0.00	0	0
Tommy Crutcher	1	5	5.00	5	0	Charlie Leigh	1	0	0.00	0	0

Ron Wolf served as the Packers' general manager from 1991-2001 and is credited with returning the franchise to the upper echelons of the National Football League. (Photo courtesy of the Green Bay Press-Gazette)

	Att.	Yds.	Avg.	LG	TD
Paul McJulien	1	0	0.00	0	0
Frankie Neal	1	0	0.00	0	0
Lester Peterson	1	0	0.00	0	0
Guy Prather	1	0	0.00	0	0
Bill Renner	1	0	0.00	0	0
Al Romine	1	0	0.00	0	0
Karl Swanke	1	0	0.00	0	0
Dave Davis	2	0	0.00	0	0
Dennis Sproul	2	0	0.00	0	0
Ray Stachowicz	2	0	0.00	0	0
Jim Lawrence	4	0	0.00		0
Doug Pederson	21	0	0.00	9	0
Jim McMahon	4	-1	-0.25	2	0
Greg Jennings	1	-1	-1.00	-1	0
JT O'Sullivan	2	-2	-1.00	-1	0
Danny Wuerffel	2	-2	-1.00	-1	0
Ken Payne	1	-2	-2.00	-2	0
Gene Wilson	1	-2	-2.00	-2	0
Herbert Goodman	4	-3	-0.75	3	0
Graham Harrell	4	-3	-0.75	0	0
Steve Bono	3	-3	-1.00	-1	0
Dennis Claridge	2	-3	-1.50	1	0
Paul Winslow	2	-3	-1.50	3	0
Bob Garrett	1	-3	-3.00	-3	0
Mark Ingram	1	-3	-3.00	-3	0
Jon Ryan	3	-4	-1.33	7	0
Dick Gordon	1	-4	-4.00	-4	0
Bobby Thomason	5	-5	-1.00	10	0
Ingle Martin	2	-5	-2.50	-2	0
Clive Rush	1	-6	-6.00	-6	0
Cal Clemons	3	-8	-2.67	0	0
Robert Ferguson	1	-8	-8.00	-8	0
Tom O'Malley	1	-9	-9.00	-9	0
BJ Sander	1	-11	-11.00	-11	0
Don Horn	12	-12	-1.00	4	1
Totals	**37851**	**148137**			**1118**

All-time 1932-2018 Receiving

Tight end Paul Coffman (82) makes a catch during the 1984 season opener against the St. Louis Cardinals. (Photo courtesy of the Green Bay Press-Gazette)

	No.	Yards	Avg.	LG	TD
Donald Driver	743	10137	13.64	85	61
Sterling Sharpe	595	8134	13.67	79	65
Jordy Nelson	550	7848	14.27	93	69
James Lofton	530	9656	18.22	80	49
Don Hutson	488	7991	16.38	92	99
Randall Cobb	470	5524	11.75	75	41
Boyd Dowler	448	6918	15.44	91	40
Antonio Freeman	431	6651	15.43	84	57

	No.	Yards	Avg.	LG	TD
Greg Jennings	425	6537	15.38	86	53
James Jones	360	5195	14.43	83	45
Ahman Green	350	2726	7.79	48	14
Davante Adams	348	4197	12.06	66	39
Max McGee	345	6346	18.39	82	50
Paul Coffman	322	4223	13.11	78	39
William Henderson	320	2409	7.53	38	14
Robert Brooks	306	4225	13.81	99	32

	No.	Yards	Avg.	LG	TD		No.	Yards	Avg.	LG	TD
Bill Howton	303	5581	18.42	90	43	John Kuhn	81	557	6.88	32	8
Carroll Dale	275	5422	19.72	89	35	Milt Gantenbein	79	1228	15.54	77	7
Dorsey Levens	271	2079	7.67	56	16	Joe Laws	79	1041	13.18		10
Gerry Ellis	267	2514	9.42	69	10	Terdell Middleton	78	659	8.45	50	3
Bubba Franks	256	2300	8.98	31	32	Al Carmichael	75	994	13.25	63	3
Edgar Bennett	242	1920	7.93	40	10	Fred Cone	75	852	11.36	69	4
Bill Schroeder	225	3435	15.27	67	20	Breezy Reid	72	868	12.06	81	5
Jermichael Finley	223	2785	12.49	62	20	Corey Bradford	71	1190	16.76	74	7
Ed West	202	2321	11.49	50	25	Antonio Chatman	71	795	11.20	25	5
Phillip Epps	192	2884	15.02	63	14	Tyrone Davis	71	780	10.99	60	13
Mark Chmura	188	2253	11.98	33	17	Herman Fontenot	71	665	9.37	59	4
Jim Taylor	187	1505	8.05	41	10	Tom Moore	71	645	9.08	45	7
Perry Kemp	182	2341	12.86	39	6	Willard Harrell	70	656	9.37	69	3
Donald Lee	178	1655	9.30	60	17	Tony Canadeo	69	579	8.39	46	5
Rich McGeorge	175	2370	13.54	51	13	Jon Staggers	65	985	15.15	63	4
Ron Kramer	170	2594	15.26	55	15	Jim Grabowski	65	575	8.85	67	3
Eddie Lee Ivery	162	1612	9.95	62	7	Jeff Query	64	902	14.09	47	4
Javon Walker	157	2444	15.57	79	22	Joe Johnson	64	652	10.19	61	4
John Jefferson	149	2253	15.12	50	11	Anthony Morgan	60	749	12.48	47	8
Keith Woodside	144	1248	8.67	49	2	Carleton Elliott	60	581	9.68	33	6
John Brockington	138	1075	7.79	48	3	Lou Brock	59	761	12.90	52	6
Gary Knafelc	134	1930	14.40	53	21	Eric Torkelson	59	469	7.95	31	0
Jackie Harris	133	1620	12.18	66	9	Andy Uram	58	1083	18.67	64	10
Paul Hornung	130	1480	11.38	83	12	Paul Ott Carruth	58	423	7.29	31	3
Howie Ferguson	127	1079	8.50	49	1	Jarrett Boykin	57	731	12.82	52	3
Donny Anderson	125	1725	13.80	51	6	Johnny Blood	56	934	16.68	70	11
James Starks	125	1017	8.14	31	6	Terry Glenn	56	817	14.59	49	2
Tony Fisher	125	900	7.20	32	5	Geronimo Allison	55	758	13.78	72	4
Richard Rodgers	120	1166	9.72	61	13	Jimmy Graham	55	636	11.56	54	2
BE Smith	120	979	8.16	42	3	Ted Cook	54	780	14.44	50	4
Robert Ferguson	116	1577	13.59	51	12	Derrick Mayes	54	730	13.52	74	5
Brandon Jackson	110	844	7.67	37	2	Keith Jackson	53	647	12.21	51	11
Bob Mann	109	1629	14.94	52	17	Harlan Huckleby	53	411	7.75	39	3
Marv Fleming	109	1300	11.93	53	12	Harry Jacunski	52	985	18.94	86	6
Ken Payne	103	1395	13.54	57	5	Ruvell Martin	52	749	14.40	36	6
Walter Stanley	101	1831	18.13	70	5	Jamaal Williams	52	472	9.08	54	2
Eddie Lacy	101	900	8.91	67	6	Clarke Hinkle	50	537	10.74	69	9
Nolan Luhn	100	1525	15.25	44	13	Travis Williams	49	530	10.82	60	5
Jessie Clark	99	925	9.34	75	6	Harry Sydney	49	384	7.84	20	1
Elijah Pitts	97	1182	12.19	84	6	Don McIlhenny	46	459	9.98	55	4
Ty Montgomery	97	827	8.53	43	3	Kenneth Davis	46	333	7.24	35	1
Vince Workman	97	691	7.12	25	5	Vernand Morency	46	311	6.76	29	0
Aundra Thompson	95	1573	16.56	57	7	Clarence Weathers	45	540	12.00	29	1
Ryan Grant	93	760	8.17	80	2	Carl Mulleneaux	44	850	19.32	56	11
Clyde Goodnight	89	1632	18.34	75	13	Brent Fullwood	44	370	8.41	67	1
Andrew Quarless	89	940	10.56	34	6	Ollie Smith	42	721	17.17	47	1
MacArthur Lane	87	855	9.83	68	4	Don Beebe	41	727	17.73	80	4
David Martin	87	766	8.80	35	9	Barry Smith	41	604	14.73	27	4
Steve Odom	84	1613	19.20	95	11	Darrell Thompson	41	330	8.05	43	1

	No.	Yards	Avg.	LG	TD		No.	Yards	Avg.	LG	TD
Ray Pelfrey	39	472	12.10	49	5	Bill Kelley	17	222	13.06	32	1
Mark Ingram	39	469	12.03	29	3	Lew Carpenter	17	213	12.53	23	0
Marquez Valdes-Scantling	38	581	15.29	60	2	Jeff Janis	17	200	11.76	46	1
Jeff Thomason	38	421	11.08	27	3	Dan Ross	17	143	8.41	16	1
Lance Kendricks	37	373	10.08	51	2	Sanjay Beach	17	122	7.18	20	1
Frankie Neal	36	420	11.67	38	3	Najeh Davenport	17	107	6.29	13	0
Reggie Cobb	35	299	8.54	37	1	Aaron Ripkowski	17	103	6.06	18	1
Aaron Jones	35	228	6.51	24	1	Nate Simpson	17	69	4.06	14	0
Aubrey Matthews	33	367	11.12	25	2	Jug Girard	16	324	20.25	75	2
Billy Grimes	32	431	13.47	96	2	Lee Morris	16	259	16.19	46	1
Mark Clayton	32	331	10.34	32	3	Jack Clancy	16	244	15.25	33	2
Veryl Switzer	31	269	8.68	28	3	Joel Mason	16	202	12.63	21	2
Jared Cook	30	377	12.57	47	1	Steve Meilinger	15	182	12.13	23	1
Noah Herron	29	211	7.28	16	2	Cecil Isbell	15	174	11.60	49	0
Al Baldwin	28	555	19.82	85	3	Justin Perillo	15	137	9.13	24	1
Patrick Scott	28	354	12.64	41	1	Wayland Becker	14	245	17.50	49	1
Koren Robinson	28	330	11.79	43	1	Dom Moselle	14	233	16.64	85	2
Michael Haddix	28	205	7.32	28	3	Ron Cassidy	14	233	16.64	43	0
John Spilis	27	446	16.52	39	1	Clive Rush	14	190	13.57	24	0
Bob Monnett	27	303	11.22		0	Larry Craig	14	155	11.07	28	0
Charles Wilson	26	389	14.96	75	1	Gary Ellerson	14	145	10.36	32	0
Leland Glass	26	380	14.62	31	1	DeShawn Wynn	14	122	8.71	18	0
Terry Mickens	26	244	9.38	24	3	Cedric Benson	14	97	6.93	18	0
Bob Long	25	487	19.48	62	4	Ben Wilson	14	88	6.29	21	0
John Hilton	25	350	14.00	65	4	Preston Dennard	13	182	14.00	34	2
Dave Hampton	25	276	11.04	50	3	LeShon Johnson	13	168	12.92	33	0
Ted Fritsch	25	227	9.08	35	1	Charles Lee	13	166	12.77	38	1
Roger Grove	24	340	14.17		3	Andre Rison	13	135	10.38	22	1
Bob Forte	24	242	10.08	28	3	Desmond Howard	13	95	7.31	12	0
Martellus Bennett	24	233	9.71	33	0	Herman Rohrig	13	94	7.23	21	0
Hank Bruder	23	344	14.96		2	De'Mond Parker	13	65	5.00	10	0
Steve Pritko	23	219	9.52	24	4	Jim Gillette	12	224	18.67	50	1
Lavvie Dilweg	22	360	16.36		2	Keith Paskett	12	188	15.67	47	1
Ralph Earhart	22	303	13.77	64	2	OE Smith	12	121	10.08	49	0
Ron Lewis	22	281	12.77	38	0	Perry Williams	12	118	9.83	24	0
Equanimeous St. Brown	21	328	15.62	54	0	Clint Didier	12	108	9.00	24	2
Al Rose	21	297	14.14		3	Carl Bland	11	164	14.91	46	1
Gary Lewis	21	285	13.57	49	1	Tory Humphrey	11	162	14.73	37	0
Korey Hall	21	137	6.52	13	1	Arnie Herber	11	155	14.09	25	2
Ray Riddick	20	285	14.25		1	Bobby Jack Floyd	11	129	11.73	44	0
Wesley Walls	20	222	11.10	36	1	Charles Goldenberg	11	111	10.09	21	1
Darick Holmes	19	179	9.42	24	0	Samkon Gado	11	82	7.45	30	1
Alex Green	19	131	6.89	19	0	Bernie Scherer	10	193	19.30	78	3
Mike Meade	19	105	5.53	31	2	Dave Davis	10	178	17.80	68	1
Tom Crabtree	18	302	16.78	72	4	Walter Tullis	10	173	17.30	52	1
Paul Miller	18	215	11.94	34	3	Bob Nussbaumer	10	143	14.30	35	0
Larry Coutre	18	202	11.22	77	2	Bill Anderson	10	119	11.90	27	1
Jim Keane	18	191	10.61	29	1	Jared Abbrederis	10	119	11.90	32	0
Steve Atkins	18	138	7.67	19	1	Dick Evans	10	111	11.10	30	0

	No.	Yards	Avg.	LG	TD		No.	Yards	Avg.	LG	TD
Randy Vataha	10	109	10.90	20	0	Hal Van Every	5	44	8.80	23	0
Brandon Saine	10	69	6.90	22	0	Terrence Murphy	5	36	7.20	12	0
Raymont Harris	10	68	6.80	12	0	Jeff Wilner	5	31	6.20	9	0
Paul Duhart	9	176	19.56	32	2	John Stephens	5	31	6.20	10	0
Charles Jordan	9	171	19.00	43	2	Quinn Johnson	5	30	6.00	11	0
George Sauer	9	142	15.78		0	Vonta Leach	5	19	3.80	9	0
Carlyle Holiday	9	126	14.00	35	0	Bill Reichardt	5	18	3.60	12	0
Brandon Bostick	9	123	13.67	26	2	Alex Urban	4	91	22.75	55	1
Andrae Thurman	9	104	11.56	33	0	Mike Moffitt	4	87	21.75	34	0
Ray Crouse	9	93	10.33	25	1	Gerald Tinker	4	84	21.00	35	1
Jim Culbreath	9	84	9.33	19	0	Robert Tonyan	4	77	19.25	54	1
Rondell Mealey	9	76	8.44	19	0	Bob Adkins	4	73	18.25	55	1
DJ Williams	9	70	7.78	12	0	Rod Gardner	4	67	16.75	33	0
Myles White	9	66	7.33	15	0	Len Garrett	4	66	16.50	21	0
Brandon Miree	9	57	6.33	20	0	Wuert Engelmann	4	54	13.50		1
Travis Jervey	9	33	3.67	11	0	Bruce Smith	4	50	12.50	36	1
Claudis James	8	148	18.50	24	2	Ben Steele	4	42	10.50	27	0
Lester Peterson	8	139	17.38		0	Michael Clark	4	41	10.25	19	0
Byron Bailey	8	119	14.88	50	0	Bill Larson	4	37	9.25	21	1
Jake Kumerow	8	103	12.88	49	1	Henry Childs	4	32	8.00	17	0
Trevor Davis	8	94	11.75	29	1	Johnathan Franklin	4	30	7.50	10	0
Larry Mason	8	84	10.50	39	1	Chuck Mercein	4	12	3.00	9	0
Del Rodgers	8	79	9.88	22	0	Fred Provo	4	-9	-2.25	3	0
Chester Johnston	8	70	8.75		1	Irv Comp	3	66	22.00	50	2
Jim Jensen	8	67	8.38	16	1	Ed Jankowski	3	65	21.67	46	1
Ryan Taylor	8	45	5.63	11	1	Allen Brown	3	43	14.33	17	0
Herm Schneidman	7	119	17.00	46	2	Marcedes Lewis	3	39	13.00	30	0
Spencer Havner	7	112	16.00	45	4	Tony Falkenstein	3	39	13.00	18	0
Jack Losch	7	85	12.14	43	0	Bob Tenner	3	38	12.67	29	0
Don Summers	7	83	11.86	17	1	Lamont Hall	3	33	11.00	13	0
Reggie Johnson	7	79	11.29	24	0	Nick Luchey	3	32	10.67	12	0
Erik Affholter	7	68	9.71	20	0	Dimitri Nance	3	30	10.00	14	0
Les Goodman	7	38	5.43	12	0	Al Norgard	3	29	9.67	22	0
Fred Nixon	6	105	17.50	32	0	Abner Wimberly	3	28	9.33	10	0
Brett Swain	6	72	12.00	31	0	DuJuan Harris	3	28	9.33	11	0
Ray Wehba	6	67	11.17	17	0	Karsten Bailey	3	26	8.67	10	0
Buford McGee	6	60	10.00	15	0	Freddie Parker	3	22	7.33	13	0
JR Boone	6	55	9.17	18	1	Kregg Lumpkin	3	22	7.33	12	0
Basil Mitchell	6	48	8.00	20	0	Ryan Wetnight	3	20	6.67	9	0
Ricky Patton	6	41	6.83	9	0	Dave Kopay	3	19	6.33	8	0
Kevin Willhite	6	37	6.17	12	0	Jim Shanley	3	13	4.33	7	0
Chuck Sample	6	35	5.83	10	1	Kapri Bibbs	3	13	4.33	5	0
Jack Cloud	6	35	5.83	13	1	Don Perkins	3	12	4.00	10	0
Terry Wells	6	11	1.83	4	0	Devante Mays	3	0	0.00	1	0
Bert Askson	5	78	15.60	34	1	Walt Schlinkman	3	-1	-0.33	5	0
Leon Manley	5	66	13.20	18	0	Don Wells	2	74	37.00	65	0
Walt Landers	5	60	12.00	55	1	Kitrick Taylor	2	63	31.50	35	1
Gene Wilson	5	57	11.40	15	0	Lavale Thomas	2	52	26.00	30	1
Dan Orlich	5	48	9.60	12	0	Don Barton	2	51	25.50	42	1

	No.	Yards	Avg.	LG	TD		No.	Yards	Avg.	LG	TD
Ed Frutig	2	40	20.00	34	0	Connie Mack Berry	1	17	17.00	17	0
Ken Keuper	2	37	18.50	26	0	Lee Weigel	1	17	17.00	17	0
Scott Bolton	2	33	16.50	18	0	Lindell Pearson	1	16	16.00	16	0
Emanuel Byrd	2	31	15.50	29	0	Harper Davis	1	15	15.00	15	0
Derrick Harden	2	29	14.50	15	0	Bill Roberts	1	14	14.00	14	0
Bob Jeter	2	25	12.50	23	0	Keith Crawford	1	14	14.00	14	0
John Thompson	2	24	12.00	23	2	Don Zimmerman	1	13	13.00	13	0
Ben Smith	2	23	11.50	13	0	Shaun Bodiford	1	13	13.00	13	0
Roell Preston	2	23	11.50	13	0	AD Williams	1	11	11.00	11	0
Larry Krause	2	22	11.00	11	0	Dick Moje	1	11	11.00	11	0
Bob Kahler	2	21	10.50	12	0	George Svendsen	1	11	11.00	11	0
Cliff Taylor	2	21	10.50	18	0	Bill Boedecker	1	10	10.00	10	0
Joe Carter	2	19	9.50	10	1	Brett Hundley	1	10	10.00	10	0
Frank Balazs	2	18	9.00	11	0	Russ Mosely	1	10	10.00	10	0
Marcus Wilson	2	18	9.00	11	0	Ace Loomis	1	9	9.00	9	0
Mike Donohoe	2	18	9.00	10	0	Syd Kitson	1	9	9.00	9	0
Patrick Collins	2	17	8.50	9	0	Ace Prescott	1	8	8.00	8	0
Chris Francies	2	16	8.00	12	0	Jeremy Ross	1	8	8.00	8	0
Frank Purnell	2	16	8.00	15	0	Lenny Taylor	1	8	8.00	8	0
J'Mon Moore	2	15	7.50	10	0	Mel Jackson	1	8	8.00	8	0
John Spagnola	2	13	6.50	14	0	Allen Lazard	1	7	7.00	7	0
Michael Blair	2	13	6.50	10	0	Mike Wahle	1	7	7.00	7	0
Aaron Hayden	2	11	5.50	7	0	Nolan Franz	1	7	7.00	7	0
Christine Michael	2	11	5.50	10	0	Ben Starret	1	6	6.00	6	0
Corey Harris	2	11	5.50	6	0	Herb Banet	1	6	6.00	6	0
Russell Copeland	2	11	5.50	12	0	James Hargrove	1	6	6.00	6	0
Ryan Krause	2	11	5.50	6	0	Val Jansante	1	6	6.00	6	0
Allen Rice	2	10	5.00	7	0	Bob Cifers	1	5	5.00	5	0
Mark Lewis	2	7	3.50	4	2	ReShard Lee	1	5	5.00	5	0
Blake Moore	2	6	3.00	3	2	Rip Collins	1	5	5.00	5	0
Jay Graham	2	6	3.00	4	0	Kevin Dorsey	1	4	4.00	4	0
Knile Davis	2	4	2.00	10	0	Bobby Collins	1	3	3.00	3	0
VR Anderson	2	2	1.00	2	0	Joe Kerridge	1	3	3.00	3	0
Tobin Rote	1	39	39.00	28	1	Danny Vitale	1	2	2.00	2	0
Dick Weisgerber	1	37	37.00	37	0	Ed Cody	1	2	2.00	2	0
Bob Summerhays	1	34	34.00	34	0	Joey Hackett	1	2	2.00	2	1
Ray Nitschke	1	34	34.00	34	0	Karl Swanke	1	2	2.00	2	1
Unaccounted for	1	30	30.00		0	Clarence Thompson	1	1	1.00	1	0
Al Cannava	1	28	28.00	28	0	Herbert Goodman	1	0	0.00	0	0
Keith Ranspot	1	25	25.00	25	1	Aaron Rodgers	1	-1	-1.00	-1	0
Jim Gueno	1	23	23.00	23	0	Bill Butler	1	-2	-2.00	-2	0
Paul Staroba	1	23	23.00	23	0	Mark Tauscher	1	-3	-3.00	-3	0
Jim Lawrence	1	21	21.00	21	0	Brett Favre	1	-7	-7.00	-7	0
Earl Gros	1	19	19.00	19	0	**Totals**	**19803**	**250008**	**12.62**		**1751**
Pete Lammons	1	19	19.00	19	0						
Walt Williams	1	19	19.00	19	0						
Cal Clemmens	1	18	18.00	18	0						
Charlie Hall	1	18	18.00	18	0						
Cornelius Redick	1	18	18.00	18	0						

All-time 1932-2018 Passing

Randy Wright prepares to pass during the second quarter of a 1986 game against the Cincinnati Bengals. (Photo courtesy of the Green Bay Press-Gazette)

	Att.	Comp.	Yards	Pct.	TD	HI		Att.	Comp.	Yards	Pct.	TD	HI
Brett Favre	8754	5377	61655	61.42%	442	286	Brett Hundley	326	194	1853	59.51%	9	13
Aaron Rodgers	5492	3560	42944	64.82%	338	80	Tony Canadeo	268	105	1642	39.18%	16	20
Bart Starr	3149	1808	24718	57.42%	152	138	Jerry Tagge	281	136	1583	48.40%	3	17
Lynn Dickey	2831	1592	21369	56.23%	133	151	Mike Tomczak	238	128	1490	53.78%	11	9
Tobin Rote	1854	826	11535	44.55%	89	119	Lamar McHan	199	81	1322	40.70%	11	14
Don Majkowski	1607	889	10870	55.32%	56	56	Bobby Thomason	221	125	1306	56.56%	11	9
Randy Wright	1119	602	7106	53.80%	31	57	Anthony Dilweg	193	102	1274	52.85%	8	7
Arnie Herber	1006	410	6749	40.76%	64	90	Earl (Jug) Girard	189	66	998	34.92%	5	13
David Whitehurst	980	504	6205	51.43%	28	51	Blair Kiel	135	80	865	59.26%	5	4
Cecil Isbell	818	411	5945	50.24%	61	52	Jim Zorn	123	56	794	45.53%	4	6
Babe Parilli	602	258	3983	42.86%	31	61	Scott Tolzien	91	56	721	61.54%	1	5
Irv Comp	519	213	3354	41.04%	28	52	John Roach	100	41	653	41.00%	4	8
John Hadl	537	280	3167	52.14%	9	29	Roy McKay	103	38	592	36.89%	6	11
Zeke Bratkowski	416	220	3147	52.88%	21	29	Alan Risher	74	44	564	59.46%	3	3
Scott Hunter	446	196	2904	43.95%	15	30	Paul Christman	126	51	545	40.48%	7	7
Jack Jacobs	442	193	2518	43.67%	21	41	Lou Brock	67	19	519	28.36%	7	5
Don Horn	284	139	2291	48.94%	16	22	Craig Nall	48	30	402	62.50%	5	0
Bob Monnett	336	158	2227	47.02%	29	26	Doug Pederson	77	46	398	59.74%	3	2
Matt Flynn	314	192	2227	61.15%	16	10	Carlos Brown	78	29	396	37.18%	3	6

Strength in Numbers

	Att.	Comp.	Yards	Pct.	TD	HI
Hal Van Every	71	23	394	32.39%	4	8
Rich Campbell	68	31	386	45.59%	3	9
Paul Hornung	55	24	383	43.64%	5	4
Jack Concannon	54	28	381	51.85%	1	3
Stan Heath	106	26	355	24.53%	1	14
Jim Del Gaizo	62	27	318	43.55%	2	6
Clarke Hinkle	53	25	293	47.17%	0	5
Vince Ferragamo	40	23	283	57.50%	1	3
Joe Francis	49	20	266	40.82%	2	3
Tom Moore	16	10	261	62.50%	4	1
Randy Johnson	35	21	249	60.00%	0	1
George Sauer	25	11	203	44.00%	1	6
DeShone Kizer	42	20	187	47.62%	0	2
Cliff Aberson	41	14	184	34.15%	0	5
Johnny Blood	41	14	184	34.15%	1	3
Don Milan	32	15	181	46.88%	1	1
Chuck Fusina	32	19	178	59.38%	0	1
Joe Laws	36	10	163	27.78%	3	6
Matt Hasselbeck	29	13	145	44.83%	2	0
Bob Garrett	30	15	143	50.00%	0	1
Seneca Wallace	24	16	139	66.67%	0	1
Willard Harrell	10	5	134	50.00%	4	1
David Beverly	6	4	129	66.67%	0	0
Elijah Pitts	9	4	113	44.44%	1	0
Frank Patrick	23	8	107	34.78%	0	2
Ty Detmer	21	11	107	52.38%	1	1
Ron Widby	2	2	102	100.00%	1	0
Herman Rohrig	9	3	100	33.33%	1	1
Mark Brunell	27	12	95	44.44%	0	0
Bobby Douglass	12	5	90	41.67%	1	1
Dennis Sproul	13	5	87	38.46%	0	0
Roger Grove	13	6	78	46.15%	0	0
Gerry Ellis	12	4	71	33.33%	1	1
Bob Forte	14	8	64	57.14%	1	1
Jerry Norton	5	3	64	60.00%	1	0
John Losch	1	1	63	100.00%	1	0
Andy Uram	7	2	60	28.57%	1	1
Hank Bruder	20	6	53	30.00%	0	2
Eddie Lee Ivery	4	2	50	50.00%	0	0
Bill Troup	12	4	48	33.33%	0	3
Ray Peterson	6	3	47	50.00%	0	0
Jim McMahon	5	4	45	80.00%	0	0
James Lofton	5	1	43	20.00%	0	0
Paul Duhart	13	4	42	30.77%	0	0
MacArthur Lane	5	3	42	60.00%	1	0
Donny Anderson	10	4	40	40.00%	2	0
T.J. Rubley	6	4	39	66.67%	0	1
Don Hutson	11	1	38	9.09%	1	2
Harry Mattos	12	4	32	33.33%	0	2
Tom O'Malley	15	4	31	26.67%	0	6
Bubba Franks	1	1	31	100.00%	1	0
Steve Bono	10	5	29	50.00%	0	0
Willie Gillus	5	2	28	40.00%	0	0
Paul Held	4	2	27	50.00%	0	0
Tim Masthay	2	1	27	50.00%	1	0
Tony Fisher	2	2	22	100.00%	1	0
Perry Moss	17	4	20	23.53%	0	0
Graham Harrell	4	2	20	50.00%	0	0
Ahman Green	2	1	20	50.00%	1	0
Fred Provo	1	1	20	100.00%	1	0
Steve Pisarkiewicz	5	2	19	40.00%	0	0
Jon Ryan	1	1	16	100.00%	0	0
Jim Lawrence	4	1	15	25.00%	0	1
Dennis Claridge	1	1	13	100.00%	0	0
Bill Stevens	5	1	12	20.00%	0	0
Joe Callahan	7	5	11	71.43%	0	0
Randall Cobb	2	1	10	50.00%	0	0
Bob Nussbaumer	1	1	10	100.00%	0	0
B.J. Sander	1	1	4	100.00%	0	0
Paul Ott Carruth	3	1	3	33.33%	1	0
Herb Banet	7	1	2	14.29%	0	2
Sterling Sharpe	1	1	1	100.00%	0	0
Charles Brackins	2	0	0	0.00%	0	0
Ernie Smith	2	0	0	0.00%	0	1
Howie Ferguson	2	0	0	0.00%	0	0
Max McGee	2	0	0	0.00%	0	1
Brian Dowling	1	0	0	0.00%	0	0
Bruce Smith	1	0	0	0.00%	0	0
Bucky Scribner	1	0	0	0.00%	0	0
Cal Clemens	1	0	0	0.00%	0	0
Carlyle Holiday	1	0	0	0.00%	0	0
Craig Hentrich	1	0	0	0.00%	0	0
Dick Bilda	1	0	0	0.00%	0	0
Breezy Reid	1	0	0	0.00%	0	0
Frank Balazs	1	0	0	0.00%	0	1
Frankie Neal	1	0	0	0.00%	0	0
J.K. Scott	1	0	0	0.00%	0	0
John Brockington	1	0	0	0.00%	0	0
Jon Staggers	1	0	0	0.00%	0	0
Paul McJulien	1	0	0	0.00%	0	0
Paul Miller	1	0	0	0.00%	0	1
Ron Kramer	1	0	0	0.00%	0	1
Russ Mosley	1	0	0	0.00%	0	0
Samkon Gado	1	0	0	0.00%	0	0
Ted Fritsch	1	0	0	0.00%	0	0
J.R. Boone	1	1	-2	100.00%	0	0
Totals	**35806**	**19826**	**250479**		**1757**	**1655**

Scoring Leaders

Points Scored by Quarter and Overtime

Punter and holder Don Bracken (right) congratulates Chris Jacke after Jacke became the first Packer to kick five field goals in a game. Jacke went 5-for-5 in a 29-16 victory over the Raiders in the Los Angeles Memorial Coliseum in 1990.

	First Quarter						Second Quarter						Third Quarter					
	TD	Att	XP	Att	FG	2-pt	Pts	TD	Att	XP	Att	FG	2-pt	Pts	TD	Att	XP	Att	FG	2-pt	Pts
Mason Crosby		141	139	65	49		286		164	162	122	98		456		116	114	82	69		321
Ryan Longwell		79	76	45	38		190		117	117	104	82		363		82	81	57	43		210
Don Hutson	22	44	41	3	0		173	42	59	55	7	4		319	14	36	32	1	1		119
Chris Jacke		64	64	43	37		175		89	87	87	65		282		70	69	48	35		174
Paul Hornung	16	43	42	36	15		183	13	54	52	42	27		211	13	38	38	31	12		152
Jim Taylor	12						72	27						162	25						150
Chester Marcol		40	35	41	25		110		51	49	74	44		181		35	34	38	26		112
Fred Cone	2	40	36	25	13		87	6	64	60	33	22		162	2	45	42	16	8		78
Jordy Nelson	17						102	22						132	14						84
Ahman Green	13						78	24						144	14						84
Sterling Sharpe	13						78	23						138	9						54
Ted Fritsch	6	8	7	35	13		82	12	21	19	36	13		130	9	19	17	13	6		89
Clarke Hinkle	11	6	6	32	8		96	12	10	8	31	11		113	9	12	10	14	6		82
Donald Driver	10						60	20						120	18					1	110
Antonio Freeman	14						84	15						90	13					1	80
Greg Jennings	10						60	17						102	15					1	92
Verne Lewellen	8						48	18						108	9						54
Max McGee	10						60	16						96	10						60
James Lofton	13						78	11						66	10						60
Jan Stenerud		28	27	13	11		60		41	40	21	15		85		20	19	13	12		55
James Jones	10						60	10						60	14					1	86
Randall Cobb	12						72	10						60	10					1	62
Dorsey Levens	7						42	15						1	92	10						60
Al Del Greco		25	25	17	12		61		30	29	25	20		89		28	28	15	8		52
Don Chandler		26	26	14	7		47		31	30	30	17		81		22	22	21	14		64
Bill Howton	11						66	13						78	6						36
Boyd Dowler	10						60	12						72	7						42
Davante Adams	12						72	8						48	7					1	44
Paul Coffman	8						48	15						90	8						48
Johnny Blood	5						30	13						78	7						43
Carroll Dale	9						54	10						60	7						42
Elijah Pitts	5						30	9						54	5						30
Gerry Ellis	4						24	9						54	13						78
Robert Brooks	13						78	14						84	6						36
Bubba Franks	5						30	10						60	10					1	62
John Brockington	6						36	13						78	6						36
Donny Anderson	9						54	12						72	4						24
Tony Canadeo	6						36	8						48	6						36
Eddie Lee Ivery	4						24	10						60	6						36
Tobin Rote	4						24	9						54	8						48
Edgar Bennett	10						60	7						42	7					1	44
Jerry Kramer		15	15	14	10		45		27	24	19	9		51		20	18	11	6		36
Eddie Lacy	7						42	7						42	6						36
Ryan Grant	11						66	11						66	1						6
Aaron Rodgers	3						18	5						30	5						30
Tom Moore	4						24	9						54	5						30
Ed West	1						6	9						54	8						48
John Kuhn	6						36	4						24	5						30
Javon Walker	5						30	7						42	5						30
BE Smith	7						42	7						42	4						24
Gary Knafelc	3						18	8						48	4						24
Joe Laws	5						30	5						30	4						24

Strength in Numbers

Fourth Quarter							Overtime				Overall Scoring						Player
TD	Att	XP	Att	FG	2-pt	Pts	TD	Att	FG	Pts	TD	XP att	XP	FG att	FG	2-pt	Points	
	138	133	111	89		400		2	2	6	0	559	548	382	307	0	1469	Mason Crosby
	102	102	68	60		282		3	3	9	0	380	376	277	226	0	1054	Ryan Longwell
27	45	43	6	2		212					105	184	171	17	7	0	823	Don Hutson
	83	81	43	34		183		3	2	6	0	306	301	224	173	0	820	Chris Jacke
20	59	58	31	12		214					62	194	190	140	66	0	760	Paul Hornung
27						162					91	0	0	0	0	0	546	Jim Taylor
	38	37	40	25		112	1	2	0	6	1	164	155	195	120	0	521	Chester Marcol
6	65	61	16	10		128					16	214	199	90	53	0	455	Fred Cone
16					1	98					69	0	0	0	0	1	416	Jordy Nelson
17						102					68	0	0	0	0	0	408	Ahman Green
21						126					66	0	0	0	0	0	396	Sterling Sharpe
8	22	19	14	4		79					35	70	62	98	36	0	380	Ted Fritsch
12	8	6	11	3		87					44	36	30	88	28	0	378	Clarke Hinkle
14					1	86					62	0	0	0	0	2	376	Donald Driver
14					1	86	1			6	57	0	0	0	0	2	346	Antonio Freeman
10					2	64	1			6	53	0	0	0	0	3	324	Greg Jennings
16	1	1				97					51	1	1	0	0	0	307	Verne Lewellen
15						90					51	0	0	0	0	0	306	Max McGee
16						96					50	0	0	0	0	0	300	James Lofton
	29	29	23	19		86		3	2	6	0	118	115	73	59	0	292	Jan Stenerud
11					1	68					45	0	0	0	0	2	274	James Jones
13					1	80					45	0	0	0	0	2	274	Randall Cobb
12						72					44	0	0	0	0	1	266	Dorsey Levens
	31	30	17	10		60		1	0	0	0	114	112	75	50	0	262	Al Del Greco
	41	39	18	10		69					0	120	117	83	48	0	261	Don Chandler
13						78					43	0	0	0	0	0	258	Bill Howton
11						66					40	0	0	0	0	0	240	Boyd Dowler
10					2	64	2			12	39	0	0	0	0	3	240	Davante Adams
8						48					39	0	0	0	0	0	234	Paul Coffman
12	1	0	1	0		73					37	1	0	1	0	0	224	Johnny Blood
9						54					35	0	0	0	0	0	210	Carroll Dale
16						96					35	0	0	0	0	0	210	Elijah Pitts
9						54					35	0	0	0	0	0	210	Gerry Ellis
2						12					35	0	0	0	0	0	210	Robert Brooks
7					1	44					32	0	0	0	0	2	196	Bubba Franks
7						42					32	0	0	0	0	0	192	John Brockington
6						36					31	0	0	0	0	0	186	Donny Anderson
11						66					31	0	0	0	0	0	186	Tony Canadeo
10						60					30	0	0	0	0	0	180	Eddie Lee Ivery
9						54					30	0	0	0	0	0	180	Tobin Rote
5					1	32					29	0	0	0	0	2	178	Edgar Bennett
	33	33	10	4		45					0	95	90	54	29	0	177	Jerry Kramer
9						54					29	0	0	0	0	0	174	Eddie Lacy
6						36					29	0	0	0	0	0	174	Ryan Grant
14					2	88					27	0	0	0	0	2	166	Aaron Rodgers
9						54					27	0	0	0	0	0	162	Tom Moore
8					1	50					26	0	0	0	0	1	158	Ed West
8						48					23	0	0	0	0	0	138	John Kuhn
5						30					22	0	0	0	0	0	132	Javon Walker
3						18					21	0	0	0	0	0	126	BE Smith
6						36					21	0	0	0	0	0	126	Gary Knafelc
7						42					21	0	0	0	0	0	126	Joe Laws

About the Author

Eric Goska

Eric Goska has been writing a by-the-numbers column following Green Bay Packers games since 1994. His unique takes on what happened on the field were published in the *Green Bay Press-Gazette* from 1994-2016 and at *Pro Football Journal* beginning in 2017.

A graduate of Northwestern University with a B.S. in mathematics, Goska demonstrated a proclivity toward numbers and the organizing of information early on. He kept a notebook as a child that listed every U.S. president, the years each served, and other facts. As a teen, he had family and friends write down the scores of ping pong games after the participants finished so he could periodically produce rankings based on winning percentages.

His love of numbers took on a football focus after being introduced to the record section of a *Green Bay Packers Yearbook* in the mid-1970s. Goska took it upon himself to come up with answers to questions such as which players had the most 100-yard rushing or receiving days.

Goska's first book, *Packer Legends in Facts*, provided a year-by-year accounting of the team, a record section with the same entries found in the *NFL's Record and Fact Book*, and a multitude of all-time lists. The work was revamped and made available in 2002 and 2003 under the name *A Measure of Greatness*.

In 1999, Goska, along with Art Daley (*Green Bay Press-Gazette* and *Green Bay Packers Yearbook*), Lee Remmel (Packers public relations director), Bud Lea (*Milwaukee Sentinel* and *Milwaukee Journal Sentinel* sports reporter) and Bob Berghaus (*Green Bay Press-Gazette* sports editor), gathered at the historic Union Hotel in De Pere, Wisconsin, to select the Packers' All-Century Team.

Goska's statistics have appeared in numerous books and magazines. Of late, he has been assisting Packers historian Cliff Christl in determining the number of games and starts made by various players.

Goska lives in Green Bay, Wisconsin, with his wife, Ann. They have two daughters: Nicole and Rebecca.

www.ingramcontent.com/pod-product-compliance
Lightning Source LLC
Chambersburg PA
CBHW081721100526
44591CB00016B/2459